COUNTERING EDUCATIONAL DESIGN

COUNTERING EDUCATIONAL DESIGN

Ted Nunan

CROOM HELM
London & Canberra

NICHOLS PUBLISHING COMPANY
New York

© 1983 Ted Nunan
Croom Helm Ltd, Provident House, Burrell Row,
Beckenham, Kent BR3 1AT

British Library Cataloguing in Publication Data

Nunan, Ted
 Countering educational design.
 1. Educational technology
 I. Title
 371.3'078   LB1028.3
 ISBN 0-7099-1812-7

First published in the United States of America 1983 by
Nichols Publishing Company,
Post Office Box 96, New York, NY 10024

Library of Congress Cataloging in Publication Data

Nunan, Ted
 Countering educational design.
 1. Curriculum planning. 2. Instructional systems.
 I. Title.
 LB1570.N86   1983   375'.001   82-24653
 ISBN 0-89397-151-0

Printed in Great Britain
by Billing & Son Ltd, Worcester

CONTENTS

1 INTRODUCTION

This book is about educational design and educational designers. It is concerned with countering a current and prevalent notion of educational design – a notion which serves the aspirations of professional educational designers who wish to create a scientific and managed form of educational practice. It is directed towards teachers and trainee teachers who are likely to meet the effects of such aspirations.

Educational Design

In the following chapters we shall consider the idea of educational design in some detail. For now, it is sufficient to point out that educational design, as it is used in this book, is a broad term which includes such things as message design, instructional design, materials design, curriculum design, and the design aspects of research and evaluation. In short, we shall be concerned with design activities which influence teaching and learning.

Design, according to Fleming and Levie (1978), refers to 'a deliberate process of analysis and synthesis that begins with a communications problem and concludes with a plan for an operational solution. The process of design is separate from the execution process'. Each of the design activities mentioned are supposed to be supported by theoretical knowledge which serves to define design as a process. But more about this later; for now, we shall try to sketch how educational design is seen by teachers and 'professional designers'.

Designing for education used to be personal, local and adaptive to differing contexts. It was practised, with varying success, by most teachers as an unselfconscious activity bound up with their role, their students, and their concept of education. Practice was varied, often idiosyncratic, and characteristically amateur. In emphasis it was qualitative rather than quantitative – decisions about design were based upon experience rather than measurement. Its evaluative standards were drawn from the settings of the school and classroom, and were readily received and recognised by other teachers in 'shop talk'.

Teachers were the educational designers. To teachers, design and planning meant much the same thing – translated to practical action it

1

meant producing lesson plans, content outlines and programmes of work for the term. Their very involvement in interpreting the syllabus meant a natural involvement with design. Often they used and produced instructional materials as a part of this design activity; a chart might be required at this point, a concept would be better explained using a picture, or perhaps a film or videotape was thought necessary. Decisions about design were not something separate from decisions made about a myriad of other concerns related to being a teacher within a particular school. That is, decisions about design were highly dependent upon circumstances such as this year's particular students, which resources were available at a particular time, or which methodologies suited a particular personal teaching style. Toomey (1977) reports much the same;

> planning like teaching method, is characterized by particularities. Much of it is idiosyncratic, particular teachers planning particular things for particular groups of students. Personal perceptions of what is appropriate for students tend to be dissimilar.

Educational design had its meaning within the teaching and learning situation of the classroom – the traditions of practice provided ways of 'making meaning' which served to inform decisions about design.

Today the trend is the reverse. Educational design has changed so much that, as a concept, it has undergone a redefinition. It now means something different. Educational design, according to the professional designer, is an activity which attempts to employ scientific approaches to design problems. Design is practised by specialist groups who, through their knowledge and practice of certain techniques, hand down the end-products of their design activities to be implemented by teachers. Courses in educational design at teacher training institutions incorporate discipline knowledge from psychology, sociology, education and the like, in an attempt to certify the practice of design. The products of educational design reach the schools in brightly coloured boxes in the form of neatly packaged curricula and audio-visual materials such as video-tapes, slide sets and multi-media kits.

Educational design is more and more practised by specialist groups such as the curriculum planner, the educational technologist and the educational evaluator. The curriculum planner works at the design of content – his brief concerns how a curriculum is designed, changed or evaluated against the background of studies in philosophy, politics, sociology and comparative approaches in education. The educational technologist centres his concern upon the production of instructional materials, and because of the interrelatedness between materials production and both curriculum and evaluation, his influence swells into these areas. The educational evaluator works at designing effective programmes of evaluation for both content and processes and, since he represents the 'quality control', his influence naturally extends throughout the whole area of educational design.

Countering Professional Design

The purpose of this book is to counter professional educational design by furthering the interests of those classroom teachers and trainee teachers who see design as an integral part of their practice as a teacher – design, to these teachers, is therefore viewed as inseparable from practice, and as such is a vital ingredient of teaching and learning. Its suggestions for practical action are motivated by the belief that the classroom teacher must retain control over design if teaching is to remain a creative, adaptive and vital undertaking.

Without the teacher in control of design, teaching for the majority of teachers will become to look more and more like the acting out of a prepared presentation – professionalised design will provide content, the sequence to present such content, determine the methodological style to be followed, provide the necessary audio-visual aids, and finally, prescribe the use of prepared checklists and tests to evaluate both the student and teacher performance.

Under such conditions teachers become more and more the consumers of packaged 'educational' products. And, just as other packaged products come with instructions for use, these educational packages have built-in instructors' manuals. Institutionalised support for the packages is often provided through in-service education, which not only instructs how to use the particular package in question, but also persuades teachers to assimilate the values behind the package approach in general. Thus, teachers will become more and more a part of a systems design in which they are assigned an implementation function.

Designers further infer a consumer status upon teachers by actively discouraging them from attempting educational design. One of the basic messages given to teachers by the educational designer is 'hands off design' and 'leave design to experts'. Also, as professionalised design represents a total plan, there is the implicit expectation that the package will not be tampered with. The reason for this is very similar to the reason that the mechanic at the authorised service centre gives Mr Average when he puts his car in for service. Piecemeal tampering or adjusting is foolhardy, as the modern car is especially designed in such a way as to prevent self-help. After being convinced of the various dangers to life and limb through self-maintenance, Mr. Average, for the sake of his and his family's well-being, relinquishes any real control over this aspect of owning a car. In much the same way the educational designer calls forth the argument that his design is the result of painstaking and thorough planning. It represents a careful orchestration of educational factors. To readjust this fine tuning may throw the package off balance to the extent of making the design ineffective. Other designers recognise the problem of teacher 'tampering' and so allow some flexibility within a fixed framework. Thus, the message is amended slightly to read 'touch only when instructed'.

Whatever the particular slant of the designer's message, one thing remains the same. Designers work towards managing the teaching and learning situation through their influence in the areas of curriculum, educational technology and evaluation. Their intent is to exert control over the activities and participants in the classroom, and they justify this by appealing to theories and techniques which are 'superior' to those possessed by teachers. Their claim rests upon the push towards more effective and efficient teaching and learning.

As managers of learning the designers can work from the strategic centre of the power structures within educational institutions. Within the school, for example, a designer can influence both the administration and the teacher when a new design calls for administrative changes to timetabling and methodological changes by the teacher. Much the same sort of thing can occur at other institutional levels. An evaluator, for example, can bring policy changes within a school authority as well as producing changes within teaching methodologies. Thus, in a very real way educational designers are middle management, and can become managers over the classroom floor.

This book works to counter the notion of design used by the professional. It contends that educational designers support particular values which establish and further their interests within institutionalised education. Such values determine the limits of educational design and contain prescriptions about how to judge 'good design'. These values knit together into a coherent position, and in order to understand their effects and eventually to counter their influence they will be examined from philosophical, political and sociological viewpoints. To focus upon these values, key questions such as 'What is educational design?' and 'Who determines what is considered to be good educational design?' are asked. These concerns are taken up in the chapters on educational design and educational designers.

The aim in writing this challenge to current notions of educational design is to present a battery of ideas and arguments which can become part of the working programme of a teacher. Thus, a good part of this work deals with how to revalue educational design from the viewpoint of the classroom floor. Basic to this revaluation is to view educational design as it was, and is, experienced and evaluated by those who produce and use it on the classroom floor. A reconceptualisation is required – present notions of educational design are structured from the position of those who would wish to manage rather than those involved in performing either teaching or learning. An alternative viewpoint from the classroom floor begins with accepting the idea that evaluative standards for design are a product of classroom life. That is, educational design as a body of knowledge must fit the educational facts with which teachers live and work.

Much of what follows deals with practical, political and philosophical points about establishing this 'classroom floor' view of educational design. The programme of this book suggests ways in which teachers and trainee teachers might practise alternatives in design within their classrooms and schools. The approach is to view design and production as a natural consequence of dealing with the curriculum and the learning situation. In practical terms the book suggests a developmental approach which grows from the use and application of 'design skills' within the particular context faced by the teacher.

Perhaps an example may make this clearer. A teacher may find the need to use an existing resource (say a photographic-slide set) in a lesson. The use of such an aid prompts analysis of the content and methodological aspects associated with this aid. The various benefits and limitations of using such an approach in the particular contextual situation are assessed by the teacher. This experience may result in a resequencing of the content (which may further lead to curriculum concerns), or a desire to supplement the materials to meet the needs of the situation (which may lead to practical problems associated with the production of photographic materials), or a feeling of dissatisfaction with previous methodological procedures (which may restructure priorities within the teaching and learning situation or perhaps change evaluative procedures).

A developmental approach is thus established within the context of where the procedures and technology are judged to be relevant. And, perhaps more importantly, such justifications are specific to the particular students and work situation of the teacher. This judgemental process leads to the development of a practical–theoretical relationship which is firmly grounded in classroom practice. To put it another way, current theoretical information ('design principles') are not taken as prescriptions, but are themselves judged in terms of their application to practice within the classroom. The chapters on countering educational design (theoretical and practical issues) attempt to establish such a dialectic relationship which can be applied to classroom life.

Countering Educational Design – a Cautionary Note

The teacher who attempts to implement the suggestions of this book will, in all probability, experience the weight of conventional wisdom concerning professionalised educational design. Perhaps a little encouragement can be taken from the fact that some educational designers, especially those within the area of curriculum, are working to reconceptualise their field. However, their efforts are largely an intellectual exercise, methodologically oriented and addressed to other professionals in the field. The burden of establishing alternative practices in design within the work-day constraints of the classroom remains with the teacher.

Thus, countering educational design is a difficult undertaking. The strategy of this book is to give suggestions about alternatives which might influence personal practice within schools. It is not concerned with how the idea of design might be changed for the professional designer; the method is to influence the personal practice of teachers rather than the group opinions of professionals.

There are three significant features of this approach by which teachers and trainee teachers might achieve some sort of personal solution within design. Firstly, the whole analysis of teaching, learning, design, classroom role and such things is unashamedly from a 'classroom-life' perspective. In fact, the suggestions towards alternatives aim to serve the interests of those involved with children at the classroom-floor level. Consequently, the analysis does not pretend to be neutral or objective – instead it is value laden, and standards and judgements are viewed from within the classroom world. Secondly, such an approach is unavoidably political – it presents ways in which teachers and trainee teachers can resist the efforts of educational designers to gain control over the area of educational design. Thirdly, this approach wishes to establish a reconceptualisation of the idea of design. It insists that evaluative standards associated with design are derived from the viewpoint of those involved in performing teaching or learning rather than from the 'world view' of those who would wish to manage teachers.

As the table of contents shows, the chapters which follow are concerned with establishing the concepts of educational design (Chapters 2, 3), analysing the values of the professional designer's ideology (Chapters 4, 5) and providing theoretical and practical counter-measures (Chapters 6, 7) in order that personal alternatives in educational design might be practised (Chapter 8).

References

FLEMING, M. and LEVIE, W. H. *Instructional Message Design*, (Educational Technology Publications, New Jersey, 1978)

TOOMEY, R. 'Teachers Approaches to Curriculum Planning: An Exploratory Study', *Curriculum Inquiry*, vol. 7, no. 2 (1977), pp. 121-9

2 EDUCATIONAL DESIGN

We have already introduced the term educational design and established its generic nature – in this book it is used to include such things as message design, materials design, instructional design, systems design and curriculum design. As each of these activities serve teaching and learning they will be included within the term educational design. Likewise, those professional educationists who specialise in any of the above are termed educational designers.

Clearly, there exist a whole range of design activities; further, within the stratifications of an education system the various 'levels' practise 'appropriate' design activities. For example, national bodies concerned with educational design are likely to restrict their immediate interest to systems rather than message design. So, given that there are a whole range of design activities within education which are carried out at differing levels, it would be reasonable to expect many descriptions of educational design. Yet the preceding descriptions were limited to two, and, as well as this, put in a somewhat stylised fashion! How can such a situation be reduced to only two *conceptions* of design?

The answer to this question involves a number of factors. For example, a discussion of the concept of design might reveal that from a philosophical analysis of 'ways of knowing' there are only two possible conceptions of educational design. At a political level, the conceptions may belong to 'controllers' and 'controlled'. At a sociological level, all those practising educational design might be considered to belong to the one and same group because they identify with (and each other by) certain special key (or core) values. But much more about such matters later. For now let us explore the situation further by looking at both the 'levels' and range of educational design.

Levels of Educational Design

At the national level bodies such as the US Institute of Education, the Australian Curriculum Development Centre, and the UK Schools Council all define their roles in educational design. The US Institute of Education, for example, provides a litany which serves to delineate the limits of current orthodoxy. In terms of Michael Apple's (1977)

8

analysis their materials can be viewed as

> affiliative (they link N.I.E. with 'the people and organisations out
> there'), as legitimating (they argue for a continuation of basically
> the same kinds of activities in which the N.I.E. has engaged in recent
> years), as prescriptive and controlling (they provide a complex,
> though sometimes non-too-subtle, series of 'clues' to people who
> want funding on what the government expects now), and as descrip-
> tive (they do in fact describe the perceptions of curricular issues held
> by some organised segments of the population, government and
> industry; if you are not organised as a lobbying force you will
> probably not be represented in these materials).

Such bodies manage the various factors of educational development –
grants, relations with private enterprise, publishing and distribution
contracts, dissemination and liaison with education authorities. Their
very existence supports the notion of educational design for efficient
and effective innovations. Further, they influence all levels of education; in Australia, for example, the federal government is involved
through its Curriculum Development Centre which, as a stated aim,
exists to foster curriculum and materials development from pre-school
to post-secondary level.

Educational designers also work within special communications
or learning divisions of large corporations. As these corporate bodies
already control the technologies, it is not surprising that they would
add to their corporate structures by creating a 'learning industry'.
Two features of this industry stand out: first, it is primarily concerned
with adapting domestic devices for education; and secondly, resource
production has, so far, lacked penetration. Not unexpectedly, profit-
ability is the key factor in development. Consequently, the education
area is seen as a sector of the high-volume domestic and commercial
market – piecemeal software development is often too specialised to
be boosted by volume sales, and therefore represents a considerable
risk. One way round this problem is to plug into national curriculum
projects or to provide packaged and comprehensive materials which,
in effect, define a curriculum. Such corporations are looking towards
selling a package of software and hardware.

The area of computer-managed or assisted instruction provides an
example of the package approach to the educational market. The
micro-chip revolution guarantees a parallel domestic market and,
because of the specialist computer language required for software

production, the education market is likely to favour packaged forms. At present System Development Corporation, Westinghouse Learning Corporation, Control Data Corporation and MITRE Corporation are all active in this area. Educational designers are producing 'curricula' in the areas of maths, reading, drama, art, music and language. Desk-top micro-computers will trigger a rebirth of educational 'programming', and educational designers are already working within the constraints of the micro-chip technology. Present micro-chip 'games-oriented' devices such as spelling-game robots, maths analysers and the like are but a foretaste of future developments.

Within a regional, state school system, or local education authority, educational designers are at work with curriculum teams and materials production officers. Service networks of education authorities involve curriculum and production specialists who work with teachers or subject committees. Traditionally, subject expertise served as the basis for authority in the area of what was to be taught and how things should be taught. However, a new superstructure has now been created where 'process' experts in design and production now oversee educational innovation.

And finally, at the school level some schools have special staffing positions which cover design, resource management and dissemination. The movement towards individualised learning through learning and resource centres has created the need for such positions. Here the designer supervises the dissemination of local or national curriculum projects, controls the development of 'in-house' curricula, manages materials production, and sometimes controls storage and acquisition of non-book resources. Occasionally, in large schools, these functions are carried out by a resource team, each member with a separate post within the school.

The Range of Design Activities

The word design can be used to describe either an *activity* or an *end point*. When used to describe an act there is the connotation of purposive deliberation about some intended activity. As an end point, the word describes the results of this deliberation. Designers involved in the act of designing eventually produce a learning and/or teaching design.

You will recall that in the introductory chapter design was defined as 'a deliberate process of analysis and synthesis that begins with a communications problem and concludes with a plan for an operational solution. The process of design is separate from the execution process'. (Fleming and Levie, 1979). Message design is therefore concerned with the purposive deliberations which go into the production of messages. A message, according to Fleming and Levie, is

> a pattern of signs (words and pictures) produced for the purpose of modifying the cognitive, affective, or psychomotor behaviour of one or more persons. The term does not imply any particular medium or vehicle of communication.

As such, 'messages' represent the 'atoms' of the communication process. Defined in this way they serve to change behaviour and so, according to behaviourist learning theory, affect learning. Many such messages, when put together in accordance with some 'logic', form the basis of instruction. One such logic, widely used by educational techno-logists and some curriculum leaders, is to structure messages according to an instructional-design plan which considers purposes, student groups, subject content, learning objectives, pre-tests, selection of teaching and learning activities, co-ordination of support services and evaluation. Such plans result from applying a systems perspective.

A systems perspective aims at describing and explaining an entity in terms of an organised complexity of mutually interacting elements (Hughes, 1979). The instructional-design plan is therefore an example of the application of the systems perspective to instruction. Systems design works to fabricate a prescriptive solution to a problem which has been analysed from a systems perspective. Curriculum design, for example, could well be attempted using the techniques of systems design.

Materials design is seen as an integral and inseparable part of message, instructional or curriculum design. Educational technologists, for example, see materials design as an aspect of message design – also, materials design and production are often major concerns for simple instructional-design models. Indeed, many of the instructional-design models which are used are selected because of their supposed ability to specify the production of materials.

One aspect of curriculum development is curriculum design. Writers in the field of curriculum are generally content to list and discuss the determinants of curriculum design. Somehow such varied and inter-active factors are evaluated and a resulting curriculum design is arrived at. Where attempts are made to be more specific about the 'design-process', models (which tend to take a systems perspective and produce a skeletal chart of the component parts and interactions) similar to instructional-design plans are produced.

Teachers and Educational Design

Having outlined both the 'levels' and range of design activities within education, it is now time to turn our attention to 'locating' the teacher within this scheme.

Now it is possible to argue that teachers have never had a role in design. Teachers, so this argument goes, have traditionally been implementers of professionalised design products – they have accepted text books and audio-visual materials prepared by experts, syllabuses prepared by subject committees, and exams devised by universities or examining boards. Now where such a situation exists it is quite true that teachers have little to do with many design tasks, and educational design becomes limited to methodologically based 'message design'. It is quite wrong to denigrate this design role – indeed, much creativity is expended in devising methodologically sound materials which serve to interpret the text and syllabuses.

But not all, and now perhaps not even the majority of teachers, find themselves in such a situation. During the last decade or so there has been a movement away from single set texts, mandatory syllabuses and standardised examinations. In many schools teachers began to design new courses, prepare accompanying media materials, and implement new forms of assessment. School-based curriculum and learning-materials development became a reality, and heralded the acceptance of a new philosophy associated with open-plan schools.

This shift in philosophy implied a greater emphasis upon student learning – in practical terms the new approach depended upon a constant supply of flexible-use learning resources. Advances in non-print technologies were to provide the means to achieving the 'open classroom'. In this situation teachers were in a unique position with regard to educational design and production. Where schools adopted this philosophy the use of individualised, resource-based, self-paced learning was encouraged, and it was the teacher who made decisions about relevant curricula, relevant materials and relevant evaluation. Design and production was personal, local and adaptive – it was an unselfconscious activity bound up with a teacher's role.

While this movement and its philosophy presented the possibility, and in many cases the opportunity, for classroom teachers to practise educational design at levels quite beyond the previous methodological approach, it was also seen by others in the education sub-culture as a means of advancement. 'Middle managers' within the school would be needed to 'control' change – in some schools a deputy principal position was allocated for this purpose. Outside the school a regional consultant would be needed to advise upon educational design, while the production of media resources would need to be centrally managed. Regional or state audio-visual centres changed their names to educational technology centres, and instead of distributing non-print resources became heavily involved in materials design. In some cases teachers objected to the whole style of management of 'their' resources by this structure, and found independent teacher centres would provide them with production facilities and a range of alternative resources. This change in philosophy can be illustrated at the school level by considering the school library. What was once a library is now the learning-resource centre; books are now a print resource, and are but one member of the family of multi-media resources.

The inclusion of non-print resources within the ambit of the library accelerated interest in the production of such resources – so much so, that some learning-resource centres are evolving into learning *and* resource centres. A learning and resource centre is distinguished by its concern for 'in-house' production and non-traditional learning services such as computer-assisted learning, counselling, remedial programmes, external studies, and diagnostic clinics – these services are in addition to, and seen as an adjunct to, the provision of a multi-media library. Consequently, such a learning and resource centre is indeed central in function and importance to an educational institution. In fact, apologists of this position argue that 'schooling' rests upon the provision of resources and instructional development services by a dedicated team of specialists. A director of such a learning and resource centre controls library and information services, media production services, an instructional design unit, and the provision of non-traditional learning services.

Similar, but less adventurous, developments have taken place in the tertiary education sector. Many institutions have instructional-development centres or tertiary teaching, research and evaluation units which provide advisory services in curriculum design, production of learning materials, course evaluation and staff development.

The Move Towards Professionalised Design

The application of new technologies in education is one factor which has drawn attention to the significance of educational design. Historically significant new technologies such as the micro-chip, the video-disc, and stationary orbit satellites put the developments of the 1980s and 1990s a 'quantum leap' ahead of the 1960s and 1970s. Such technologies are not 'more of the same'. Instead, they promise a new set of assumptions about the partnership between education and technology; educational designers will help to celebrate a marriage between the two.

Take for example, the video-disc. Magnavox's *Magnavision* system has a capacity of some 54,000 still pictures or 60 minutes of television programme per side of disc. Discs will eventually sell for about the same price as a long-playing (audio) record.

Obviously there is a huge potential for the application of such discs to the education market. But there are also grave dangers associated with this trend – just as the ordinary citizen is unable to produce an audio-disc recording (unlike the production possibilities inherent in the ordinary home-market cassette recorder) the teacher has no 'production possibilities' with the video-disc. Consequently, the teacher is put in the position of either using materials as resources (i.e. selecting sections of various programmes and so attempting to retain control over instructional and curriculum design) or accepting materials as a package. Such difficulties with carrying out production (which, for teachers, makes design in this technology out of the question) means that design is 'centralised' and mass market in approach. Similarly, the possibility of low-cost distribution of TV via satellite could result in a 'rationalisation' of course offerings where a single institution beams out 'instruction' to a number of classes. The newer technologies, design-wise, have a centripetal tendency – and often this aspect is glossed over, stressing instead a projected diversity of 'centralised' design. Whatever their future impact, one thing is certain: such technologies are sure to foster the values behind professional educational design.

Another factor which works to thrust professionalised educational design into classroom life is 'accountability'. Public pressure for accountability of public expenditure means that schools and other educational institutions have had to face, and, in anticipation, ask of themselves, questions relating to the 'value' of their programmes. Some of the fuel for this trend towards accountability is provided by slow or no-growth economic conditions – the constant pressure for innovations now means that change occurs by rearrangement and reallocation rather than expansion. Such conditions foster a 'what can be counted, counts' attitude towards education. That is, in order to be able to rearrange and reallocate in a cost-effective fashion, the first step is to 'quantify' so that 'objective' comparisons can be made. Instructional accountability thus comes to be defined in terms of providing clearly stated objectives, detailed plans for achieving such objectives, and developing evaluative mechanisms for comparing the actual results of instruction with the pre-set objectives. A circular relationship sets itself up: instructional accountability fosters 'professionalised' educational design which in turn strengthens the accountability trend.

Many teachers feel uncomfortable about the scrutiny that such a trend brings. This feeling results from the belief that 'accountability' studies will use criteria which relate to management and efficiency rather than classroom-oriented measures of variables like interpersonal interaction and student involvement. For example, the criteria of instructional accountability mentioned above are derived from a management interpretation of teaching and learning with which many teachers are unfamiliar – and, where teachers are unsure, or can be made to feel unsure of their abilities in stating objectives, planning, and evaluation, the pressure to solve this accountability threat by resorting to professionalised design is high. Also, the designers argue that school administrators can feel safer with professional design products, as they are often empirically field-tested and amended before production. A further point in their favour is that such packages often have inbuilt evaluative mechanisms which allow control and accountability at the school level.

Also, teachers see such 'accountability' as a threat to their professional status. Whitfield (1974) puts it this way:

When teachers close the door of the classroom . . . and lessons begin, they enter the private interactive world of relationships between themselves, their subject matter and their pupils. They cease in many ways to be readily accountable to parents, colleagues and other educational personnel, let alone politicians and voters, for they recognise that their teaching space is by tradition sacrosanct, that it is, or can be, firmly insulated from outside observation and interference . . . In the classroom teachers are unavoidably extensive choice-makers in their own right, and this is a central component of the concept of professionalism which makes teachers significantly different from technicians.

Educational designers restrict or remove 'choice' on the classroom floor by management of processes (curriculum, educational technology and evaluation) which ultimately affect classroom life.

The designer argues for his role and product by citing what he sees as the unique benefits of professionalised design. First and foremost there are the matters of efficiency and effectiveness – instruction, because of the extensive and careful design, will become a secure undertaking, and results will improve. Further, because of the proper support in the form of audio-visual aids, devices and resources the package will improve student interest in the topic. The classroom will be transformed – willing learners will be assisted by organised teachers. Indeed, in using the designer's products the teacher's approach displays long-term organisation towards identifiable goals. The teacher will now appear more 'professional' and, as designers well know, appealing to the 'professionalism' of teachers cannot fail.

As the teacher does not have the worry of design and materials production, the designers argue, he can now use this gained time to provide greater individual attention to the individual differences of students. Teaching, therefore, becomes a more enjoyable, rewarding and valuable occupation. Teachers, so this line of argument goes, can now devote their undivided attention and energies to fostering 'communication' within the classroom.

Another technique the designer uses to establish his role and products is to make teachers feel inadequate in the area of design. Designers point to teachers not knowing certain techniques, or suggest that the teachers are unable to keep up with current trends and equipment. But, above all, designers stress the fact that teachers just do not have the time to devote to such matters. For this reason, and often this reason alone, designers argue for their role within an educational system. But, as many teachers point out, this argument counts for little. It is a fact that teachers rarely have time which is officially allotted for educational design within schools – but this situation is 'political', as it could be changed by employing more teachers so that each could now have time to become involved with design.

Teacher Attitudes Towards Professional Design

Teachers and trainee teachers have different attitudes towards this design trend, depending upon how they interpret the promise offered by the designers. Some, the technological progressives, see professionalised design as a natural outgrowth of the application of such technologies as video and micro-chips to education. That is, it is the technologies themselves that have brought and accelerated the need for a professional approach to educational design. Further, this group views this movement with approval; the new technologies will supposedly provide the instruments for educational advancement to liberate children and teachers alike from the distasteful and routine aspects of teaching and learning. Education, through the use of such technologies, will be fun. Schools will become social, cultural and entertainment centres, and learning will be carried out, upon demand, at home. Teaching becomes 'guiding the social development of the child'!

Other teachers strongly oppose this 'romantic' vision. They argue that the technologies and techniques do not spell liberation – in fact, they point to the reverse. Educational designers, through their control over technologies and techniques, infringe upon the personalised texture of the classroom. They remove or prevent many of the things that teachers value most within their classroom.

New technologies are not merely good or bad depending upon their use – instead, they carry with them hidden assumptions. The very act of using such technologies has inherent consequences. For example, the idea of utilising advertising techniques for children's television in Sesame Street has, in the opinion of many teachers, resulted in the children absorbing the forms of advertising and television as well as the content. Children have become attuned to the short, non-sequential approach of presenting such programmes, and find difficulty in sustaining attention in school. Another example is provided by the case of programmed learning; here again, it was the form of the technology and technique (independent of teaching machine or book form or linear or branched programme) which was regarded as undesirable.

Other teachers view the effects of this movement on a quite different level. Their concern is for themselves rather than the 'system'. They take it as given that the educational-design movement will permeate schooling, and are concerned with the possibilities that this trend presents for personal advancement within the educational system. The trend carries with it the need for a new group of middle managers within either the educational authority, subject discipline group or school. Such positions present promotion opportunities. Not unexpectedly, for such teachers the movement towards professionalised design is a good thing and can be fully justified, in their view, by the calls for more efficient and effective management of teaching and learning. The band-wagoners ride the gravy train!

Conceptions of Educational Design – Two or More?

It is now time to return to the question which was posed at the beginning of the chapter. Clearly, there are a whole range of design activities
within education which are carried out at differing levels – so why not
provide a stylised portrait of each of these?

To answer this question we need to consider the purpose of this
book. The following chapters attempt to provide teachers with information and techniques which counter educational design at the teaching
and learning level of the classroom. Counter-measures are therefore seen
at the level which is most immediate to teachers – that is, what will be
called a 'middle-management' level.

There are many related reasons for applying a dichotomous split to
the concept of educational design, and the next chapter analyses the
concept of educational design in order to establish these reasons.
However, to foreshadow the argument of the next chapters the position
taken in this analysis is that educational design is inextricably bound
up with the notion of management. Either one is a controller or is
being controlled; consequently there is a conception of educational
design which belongs to the controllers and another for the controlled.
Now (excluding, for the moment, students) the teacher is seen as 'the
end of the line' with regard to management of teaching and learning.
So, relative to the teacher (who, by this scheme, is 'controlled') all
other positions of the educational hierarchy which concern themselves with this area must be 'controllers'. Therefore, for the purposes
of this book all design levels work from the *value position* of a controller and cast the teacher (and student) as controlled.

The following chapters attempt to establish this position by illus-
trating *value positions* rather than actual cases of middle management.
The approach is sociological, and based around the notion of key or core
values held by groups. Teachers should, therefore, be able to identify the
ways in which they are being managed (through values) and who is
attempting to manage them (by those who hold such values).

The next chapter is concerned with the concept of educational
design which is examined from the value positions of both professional
designers and teachers.

References

APPLE, M. 'Politics and National Curriculum Policy', *Curriculum Inquiry*, vol. 7,
     no. 4, (1977) pp. 355-61.

FLEMING, M. and LEVIE, W. H. *Instructional Message Design*, (Educational Technology Publications, New Jersey, 1978)

HUGHES, A. S. 'The Potential of Systems Philosophy for Theory and Research in Curriculum', *Programmed Learning and Educational Technology*, vol. 16, no. 3, (1979), pp. 195-9

WHITFIELD, R. 'Teachers' choices and Decisions Inside the Classroom', *Australian Science Teachers' Journal*, vol. 20, no. 3, (1974), pp. 83-90

3 ANALYSING EDUCATIONAL DESIGN

Teachers and professional designers provide two different sets of characteristics associated with educational design. How can it be that two opposed positions both claim to describe educational design? Can we decide whether one view is right and the other wrong? Is it possible that both views are equally relevant yet describe different facets of the same thing? Could it be that both views are imperfect yet one view decidedly superior?

It should be made quite clear from the outset that it is the concept (or concepts) of educational design that is under scrutiny. The analysis is therefore not restricted to any particular level or type of design within the range of activities. However, as the purpose of this book is to provide ways to counter educational design from the class-room floor, the analysis in this chapter will relate to the aspects of educational design which have a direct bearing upon classroom life. Consequently, the examples which illustrate the professional's concept of design relate to school-based concerns such as curriculum-unit design, instructional-systems design (the school or groups of schools as a system) and message design.

The Game of Educational Design

Before starting an analysis of the concept of educational design let us make a couple of procedural rules. First, we will agree to stop a particular line of inquiry if things look as if they are likely to lead to equally or more complex considerations. That is, the particular tack of an argument must look as if it is becoming 'convergent', and show possibilities of clarifying rather than confounding issues associated with educational design. In this way we hope to avoid wandering for too long down potentially less fruitful pathways. Although this approach is unsatisfactory in that it suggests avoiding 'in-depth' discussion, we will probably take up many of the temporarily discarded issues in later chapters.

Secondly, we start from the fact that the concept of educational design differs according to its use by two groups – teachers and professional designers. Differences in the way that each group 'defines' or 'makes meaning' of the term are like a set of rules of a game. The players which employ concept A work out their strategies and play under rule-set A; the players employing alternative strategies and playing under rule-set B follow concept B. Now this situation could well characterise educational players involved with design – teachers might well be those using rule-set A while professional designers rule-set B. We of course assume that rule-set A and rule-set B are not so dissimilar that they define two distinctly different games!

To analyse the idea of educational design we will first assume that some universal concept and rule-set exists – that is, our task will be to assume the position of independent unbiased observers and 'discover' (or perhaps uncover) this rule-set. As observers we see rule-sets A and B as adaptations of the universal rule-set. The adaptations are the result of each group of 'players' bending the universal rules to suit their circumstances. Consequently, we might well reconstruct the 'universal' concept and the rule-set by 'unbending' the competing conceptions. We therefore begin by 'umpiring' the arguments about educational design put forth by these two groups. This approach might help distil a single meaning of the term educational design, or alternatively expose the impossibility of 'umpiring', as we may well find that no universal concept or rule-set exists.

To extract the rule-sets from these competing conceptions of educational design we return to the questions that we first posed. Can we decide whether one view is 'right' while the other wrong? Is it possible that both views are equally relevant in that they describe different facets of the single reality? Could it be that both views are imperfect yet one view decidedly superior?

In order that we can seek relevant answers to such questions we must first refine them. To do this it is necessary to specify a common ground to which the questions relate – this area is the *design in action*. This concept can best be explained by looking at the purposes behind educational design.

A teacher's view of educational design begins and ends with reference to the classroom floor. A design is a product of somebody's or some group's purpose. Often, a design serves the purposes of an individual teacher, and the materials and processes which represent the design in action are intended for no other teacher or classroom. This situation contrasts strongly with 'professional' design, where the purposes behind the design are to prescribe both processes and products for mass consumption by teachers and students.

Now these two purposes appear different – one aimed at particularities, the other at servicing the widest possible market. Yet in terms of the *design in action*, both approaches involve students and teachers dealing with processes and materials at the classroom level. This situation is graphically illustrated by the case where 'professional design' and 'teacher design' are involved with the same content. The intent of the teacher is to design teaching and learning materials which serve his purpose and his children. Likewise, the professionalised design, in action, will be working upon the very same children in the very same classroom. Presumably they are both working to inform, instruct, build attitudes and a host of other objectives thought applicable in the subject area.

The point that is being made here is that the values behind conceptions of design will be evaluated in terms of the acts of teaching and learning, not of management and bureaucracy. This stance is based upon the belief that the whole purpose of educational design is to facilitate teaching and learning, and, in the last analysis, this stands or falls at the level of classroom life. However, for the moment, let us suspend this belief and attempt to explore these questions, keeping in mind the 'acid test' of common ground derived from considering the 'design in action'.

Let us first ask whether both groups can be equally right in their distinct views about educational design. One logical consequence of a 'yes' answer to this question is that the conceptions each describe different parts of 'educational design'. In terms of our rule-set characterisation, this would mean the 'universal concept' would be formed from the sum of rule-set A and rule-set B. A political consequence of accepting that both views could be equally right is that direct confrontation between the two groups involved in educational design is avoided.

Now is there any way of deciding whether both groups have equally correct views? Perhaps a look at the claims of the professional designer may help. Professional designers insist that their design activities are very different from those which teachers carry out. Indeed, the two groups engage in activities which are so distinctly different that, according to the designers, they should not be mixed together.

Long-range vs Short-range Purposes

The reasoning behind this depends upon a separation of purpose which they describe by the terms 'immediate' and 'long-range'. The immediate aspects of design are characterised by preparation of lesson plans some hours before a lesson begins. It is a 'short-range' activity in that the design is seen as piecemeal and concerned primarily with implementation. Implementation is the word used for 'doing' a lesson – other favourite terms, which are often substituted, are presentation and delivery. So according to educational designers, teachers carry out design as a hand-to-mouth activity.

Designers, on the other hand, see themselves as properly concerned with long-range purposes which are decidely more complex and varied. Design, in this case, is much further removed from implementation, and is clearly not the same type of activity which teachers practise.

But professional designers add one thing more. Teachers, so their reasoning goes, should not be taken from their prime function of classroom presentation. To expect them to cope with the arduous circumstances of the classroom and, as well, to be involved with long-term design is unreasonable. Consequently, a neat division of labour into professionalised design and implementation is necessary. We therefore find the designers appealing to the following sort of statement about design:

> (previously) we have had to place the responsibility for effective instruction completely upon the teacher, rather than dividing that responsibility into a design responsibility and an implementation responsibility. But now we do have the educational philosophy and the supporting technology that can be used (Deterline, 1968)

So educational design, according to this view, has two 'design' phases – an 'immediate' and a 'long-range' phase. Since these two phases are markedly different in purpose and effect, it is not surprising that two conceptions of educational design should exist – two sets of different rules and strategies are seen to cover the two phases. The professional designer works to ensure that his conception, that of long-term design, is the dominant view.

But can we agree that there are two phases to educational design? Is what the teacher does merely a matter of minute-to-minute, hand-to-mouth design? Surely a lesson plan is not conceived as a single, un-connected, discrete happening! Teachers do connect their design with a larger purpose – a lesson plan is conceived with a mind to the preceding and future lessons. It is true that design as carried out by teachers is rarely intended for other teachers or for commercial pro-duction, but this does not mean that such design is not long term.

So, what are made out to be separate and distinct phases (and tasks appropriate to each phase) might not be all that different.

The Systems Approach

Now if there are not two separate phases representing mutually exclusive activities, suppose both teachers and designers were, in fact, carrying out the one and same activity. Both groups would have the same task, but differ in how to go about getting the job done. Can we then decide upon which view of design is superior?

The professional designer again has a ready answer. He returns to the position that his design activities are different and distinguishable from that of the teacher due to his scientific and systematic approach. This approach, which employs a body of theoretic knowledge and practical techniques, is supposedly able to solve design tasks more effectively and efficiently. Such principles and techniques are not necessarily derived from classroom practices, but instead employ theoretical studies in psychology (such as information processing, behaviourism) communications, media and so on. In short, educational design has become 'scientific'. Not only do the basic strategies such as systems approaches ape the so-called scientific method, but the 'principles of design' are supposedly scientifically derived from the 'educational sciences'.

In contrast, the approach of the teacher is seen as primitive – according to the designer it is characterised by a dependence upon intuitive, personalised and subjective information which necessarily means ineffective, piecemeal and unorganised attempts at educational design. The efficient design of the professional designer is therefore a consequence of superior knowledge and technique.

This contrast is illustrated by the well-worn example of estimating the trajectory of a cannon ball. One approach is to apply Newton's formula which describes the trajectory – theoretically, the exact landing point can be determined when we know the muzzle velocity of the cannon ball, the angle at which the cannon is fired and the value of the gravitational constant for the area. The other approach is to fire the cannon a number of times and observe the changes in distance with angle.

While the first may seem theoretically powerful and preferable to the 'trial and error' of the second approach, it is not quite that simple. This is because the theoretical predictions are based upon assumptions which do not apply in the real world. First, the cannon ball is not moving in a perfect vacuum but through a viscous fluid, air; secondly, the cannon ball, in all probability, has received some spin and this will affect the trajectory; thirdly, the ball is not perfectly spherical in shape and so presents aerodynamic problems; fourthly, the prevailing winds will influence the trajectory.

Is it possible to decide which approach is superior? And, we might well ask, superior in what way? The fact that there are theories which deal with the movement of objects through viscous fluids or the deviation caused by circular motion and so on may count for little – as a practical problem it may well be impracticable to work with such complex considerations. Thus, the second approach based upon observations of the trajectory may be equally effective.

Now with this example it is possible to examine the merits of each approach. Here the theoretical approach depends upon a number of different, well-established theories – the complexities of computation can be managed by computers. But what happens when we consider these two approaches within the field of education instead of the field of battle?

Where are the educational theories which are able to explain and predict? Are the situations and variables so easily defined? Is there some science of education which can be applied in the same way that the area of dynamics 'predicts' the trajectory of the cannon ball?

Within the area of educational design such doubts lead us to ask just how much or how little of educational design is assisted by 'scientific' principles of design. That is, can we believe the argument put forth by professional designers? Kenneth Richmond (1972), in writing about the place of media in educational design puts this concern for principles derived from theory in the following way:

Which media can most appropriately be used to achieve given learning objectives? What are the peculiar properties of motion film with or without a sound track, of black and white *vis-à-vis* colour film, of film strip, of slide-tape, of wall charts? How does film differ from television? When is recorded sound more powerful than a visual image? These and a host of related questions concerning the 'grammar' of the various media are now increasingly exercising the minds of educational technologists. How to bring all the *disjecta membra* together under the roof of an overarching theory which will be at once descriptive, explanatory and predictive? That is the question.

Indeed, to view educational design as a scientifically based study infers the existence of some overarching theory which, because of its descriptive, explanatory, and above all, predictive nature, provides the designer with principles of design. Unfortunately, no such theory exists, and consequently the push for a science of instruction is made on grounds which are questionable. Indeed, we could speculate that the 'scientific approach' provides concepts and metaphors which create an aura of technological rationality which is used to confer professional status and exclude the uninitiated! We therefore return to the problem of deciding whether there is any way of making a decision about the designer's claim of better and more efficient design through superior knowledge and technique.

While 'educational design' itself is not derived from an overarching theory, it is seen to be allied to 'scientific' approaches through what is called the 'systems' approach. This approach will be investigated in some detail in a later chapter. However, for now, we describe the systems approach as a way of looking at a process - its methodology is to break down a whole into its components, and then chart the interrelations between these components in order to use the whole to solve some problem. As one writer puts it, it is a technique which allows us to take a good look at the forest before hacking away at the trees.

A good way to introduce the idea of systems is to take a concrete example - a motor cycle. A 'systems' perspective begins by making an analytic description - a cycle becomes a number of component assemblies each having a function.

The motor cycle is conceptually 'carved-up' into its sub-systems to produce a hierarchical structure. The first carve-up is to see a motor cycle as a power assembly and a running assembly. The power assembly is further divided into an engine and a power-delivery system; the engine is comprised of a fuel–air system, an ignition system, a feedback system, a power train and a lubrication system. In a like fashion the running assembly can be analytically divided up.

So much for the components. The other part of a systems explanation deals with the ways that the various sub-systems interact with each other. For example, the fuel–air system and the ignition system interact, and so on.

Now once this 'carving-up' is completed it is possible to *use* the structure in a special way. One of the purposes of conceptualising the motor bike in this way is to be able to 'control' it.

The structural division helps to relate any sub-system to the whole, and so changes or faults in any sub-system can be charted through the various interactions and recognised as 'symptoms' in the reactions of the whole. Thus a 'spluttering' of the engine is seen in terms of a fault in one of the sub-systems A, B or C and not in D, E or F.

Thus, systems perspectives are linked to problem-solving. The analytic structure defines a particular approach to problem-solving – an approach which is formalised in the so-called scientific method. This approach is characterised by a number of sequential steps – the statement of the problem, the hypothesising as to the cause of the problem, the carrying out of empirical experiments to test such hypotheses, predicting the results of experiments, observing the results, and finally drawing conclusions. This problem-solving sequence allows 'control' in two ways. First, where the system is not functioning correctly it provides a powerful way of fault-finding, and allows the re-tuning of the system: secondly, it provides an understanding of the properties of the system so that changes to various sub-systems can be designed in order to produce a new system.

Application of this systems perspective to design for teaching and/or learning is heralded as an important educational advance. For example, it serves to provide a means of organising and applying knowledge about design problems. In the area of design this approach provides a basis for making 'educational hypotheses' in the form of statements about observable student behaviours. That is, lesson objectives are pre-set as hypotheses about behaviours which should appear after an 'educational experiment' called instruction. Educational design supplied the 'principles' (or 'theories') which predict outcomes while the teacher, through presentation of the design, empirically tests the hypotheses. For those who like analogies, doing the scientific experiment becomes the classroom implementation, the scientist the educational designer, the laboratory technician the teacher, and the hypothesis and experimental technique the educational design.

But more about the systems approach later. For now we note that a systems perspective has been applied to the teaching and learning situation which has been analytically carved up, in various ways, into its sub-systems. Systematic approaches to individualisation of learning, teaching, instruction, secondary education, materials production and curriculum development are but some of the common examples which come to mind.

In summary, the designers' claim to superior knowledge and technique is based on the way the systems perspective allows the application of scientific 'knowledge' and 'method'. If scientific method defines a rational way to go about problem-solving in science, then the systems approach is its educational counterpart. Thus, rational design is guaranteed with the systems approach; other approaches are, almost by definition, inferior.

There have been, however, many challenges to the superiority of scientific rationality – and it is by no means certain that the designers' claims of superiority can be adequately based upon such grounds. Further, we cannot be at all sure that techniques which are applied in the sciences are applicable or even relevant to educational problems.

So far we have been unable to answer two questions. The quest to decide whether both groups have equally valid views exposed a division of labour disguised in terms of 'long-term' and 'short-term' phases of educational design. And the attempt to decide which view might be superior pointed towards a long and involved debate about the status of 'scientific' and 'non-scientific' knowledge. Let us change the tack of our investigation and consider the two aspects of teachers who undertake courses in educational design and the acceptance of professional design products. Both of these avenues provide insights into the 'world views' of both teachers and professional designers.

Teachers who Undertake Courses in Education Design

The following two chapters detail information which establish the 'world view' of professional education designers. However, before we enter into these specialist 'world views' through the professional designer's own characterisation of his role and influence, we can gain significant insights into these 'world views' from teachers who undertake courses in educational technology or curriculum. Such teachers already possess a working notion of educational design. This notion is formed from, and consistent with, a particular construction of reality – theirs is a notion which fits classroom life.

Teachers take such courses expecting that this classroom notion of educational design will be sharpened and extended – however, they soon realize that courses in educational technology and curriculum attempt to change their 'world view'. And teachers are extremely sensitive to what it is that is being changed!

What is especially significant is that this group questions two aspects of the professional's view. The clarity and precision with which teachers identify these two issues suggest that they are significant anomalies – both issues clearly pose contradictions to the teacher's reality. Thus, both these aspects serve to highlight the differences between the working notion of design that teachers bring to such courses and the different notion of design taught within the course. The two issues concern the 'range' and 'blank-slate' aspects of design.

To outline why teachers consider these two related aspects as highly significant, let us look further into their interpretation of professional design. Teachers report that design as conceptualised by professionals is the pre-planning of a preferred course of action which is to be carried out by others. Design principles allow pre-planning – that is, they provide means for making choices about the way to proceed. The design itself, therefore, represents an expectation of the teaching and learning activities that should actually occur; it also provides an expectation of what types and of how much learning will occur.

The purpose of a design is to prescribe action for others – that is, the procedures employed to justify a design exist because of the fact that a design has 'potential users'. A design therefore requires acceptance by others – the 'scientific' nature of the principles is an attempt to persuade others to accept the reasoning behind a particular design.

Now both the 'blank-slate' and 'range' aspects are related to this conception of design. To see the importance of these assumptions let us look at what happens to the notion of design if the assumptions do not apply.

Suppose design as practised by professionals had to be carried on within a fluid and on-going situation – that is, the designer has a much restricted control over the choices available to him. Indeed, the choice and control over genuine alternatives for action might be so limited that any appeal to theoretic knowledge would appear pointless! In fact, in this situation practical knowledge based upon experience might prove more useful.

So the first point that teachers make is that the use of theoretical knowledge requires a situation to which this information is 'sensible'. The easiest possible way to structure such a circumstance is to remove all the practical constraints and, as a part of the design, define the exact conditions for the success of the design. Thus, in order to use theoretic knowledge the designer insists upon working from a 'blank slate', and then specifies the working conditions of the design within the overall package. An essential feature of this approach is therefore a rejection of the 'world view' of the teacher – classroom life is to fit design and not the other way round!

Now let us consider the 'range' aspect. What does it mean to speak of the range of a design? And what are the consequences of rejecting the long-range assumption?

The range of a design often refers to two related things – its breadth and quantity of potential users and the scope and depth of the planning within the design. The standard assumption made is that designs with considerable scope and depth attract a larger number of users. Or, as a practical point, the attraction of a larger number of users means that a design must display scope and depth. To justify the existence of professional designers and the considerable time, funds, and energy expended in designing, the range of a design must be long rather than short.

What are the consequences of rejecting the long-range assumption? Long-range design as a prescriptive activity depends upon the acceptance of the superiority of theoretic knowledge in guiding design. Without this acceptance the whole notion of long-range design and indeed the need for such an activity is called into question. To put it another way, short-range design employs standards of justification which are more personal, context dependent, and practical – the very concept is opposed to the management intent behind long-range design. Long-range design cannot avoid the 'economics' of its very existence – since it is directed towards others a 'cost-effectiveness' return is required of the design.

This aspect of 'cost-effectiveness' introduces a further characteristic of professionalised design. Its success in affecting a particular student or a special group of students is incidental – its acceptance is measured in terms of mass use. Consequently, much is at stake, and there is a considerable investment in establishing a superior status for such professionalised products. Also, a whole range of persuasive techniques are employed in an attempt to induce wide usage.

Accepting Professional Design Products

A significant part of the role of the professionalised designer is, therefore, to persuade potential users into accepting the design. A converse of this is to dissuade teachers from carrying out their own educational design. For every teacher involved with design there is possible one less to consume professionalised design!

Where designers have not infiltrated the institutionalised education system the various brochures advertising their materials are careful to include the very latest educational jargon. The Walt Disney group, for example, claim that their materials enhance students' self-confidence and give individualised practice – in a nutshell, the Disney materials, so we are told, represent 'those little rewards that enrich the classroom . . . [producing] an ideal incentive for positive behaviour reinforcement'. (Disney Catalogue, 1977) Special teachers' guides launch ideas for classroom discussion, role-playing and the teaching and learning activities. Teachers are exhorted to discover how Disney makes subjects easier to teach and more fun to learn using 'enthusiasm to develop a high-powered learning experience'. The slogans are endless, and reinforce the notion that Disney provides the 'magic' for students; the teacher (through the Disney teacher's guide) brings together the ingredients, the students and the materials design, under the special prescribed conditions.

The Disney approach is to provide materials which deal with the 'central' concepts of curriculum (or cross-subject) areas. Thus, the educational designer produces orchestrated 'Disney Magic' for safety, health, guidance, holidays, social studies, language-arts, reading, communications, science, nature studies, music and special education. This magic is, not unexpectedly, available to all – the brochure takes pains to point out that every youngster will experience gripping excitement, grasp principles, discover (or whatever), because Disney designers arrange clear and simple 'lessons'. Even the teacher's guide is 'easy-to-understand' and 'non-technical', thereby including every teacher as a potential user!

This problem of persuasion is made easier when designers work within institutionalised settings. Here curriculum leaders and educational technologists become part of the bureaucratic structure of institutionalised education. The obvious advantage of this is that the role of the professional designer is already recognised by the bureaucracy, and the design gains the weight of bureaucratic authority and its use becomes 'mandatory' within the structure.

In such settings the success of a design becomes, in part, a function of success within a bureaucratic system. This, in turn, influences design – for example, the designer will be better received within this system if his own approach to design employs techniques which are approved by, or complement, the system. Because of this, theoretical stances which define design in terms of questions amenable to answer by modern bureaucracies have considerable influence.

Professional Educational Design as Ideology

So far we have investigated two features of the concept of design employed by professional designers – firstly a design must be seen in terms of theoretic rather than practical knowledge, and secondly, a design represents a prescribed and managed course of action which is 'public' rather than 'private'. The other two issues of teachers involved in courses in educational design and the acceptance of professionalised design also point to a coherent 'world view' which carries a host of social, political and economic assumptions about educational design. And since these assumptions belong to a particular group, we therefore begin to view the idea of design as an ideology.

So far, using the word ideology has been avoided and since the meaning of the word is open to considerable interpretation it is necessary to clarify the way that it will be used here. The word 'ideology' is often used to refer to a system of beliefs held by a particular class or group. There is also the inference that in linking such beliefs with social groups the existence of the group (and the furthering of the group's interests) is a function of the ideology. Also, it is evident that the term can also refer to the way that 'meanings and ideas' are produced for a social group. An ideology enables an interpretation of events or situations and assists in choices for individual and group action. A fundamental part of an ideology is the values which are central to the belief system held by the group. Sometimes the word ideology is used to assess such belief systems, and in such cases the label often infers a system of false or illusory beliefs.

When ideology is used here the meaning will concern both the 'sense-making' and the 'social group and individual interest' aspects. Ideas and knowledge by being included within an ideology are not necessarily false or insincerely held. Thus, we are not concerned as much with the latter 'false-consciousness' aspect of the term as with the dual aspects of 'meaning or sense-making', and maintaining or furthering the interests of the group and its members.

Linking design with ideology is to focus upon the 'meaning-making' and 'social-interest' functions of the design concept within the social groups of the professional designers and teachers. The existence of two notions of design suggests two distinct ideologies concerned with the role of teachers and designers in education.

But the idea of design itself does not constitute an ideology. We are faced now with the fundamental question of what constitutes the essential beliefs held by these social groups. Such beliefs serve to identify membership of specialist groups – indeed, we might say that a central core of beliefs have a group existence in that individuals cannot contravene them and remain within the group.

Beliefs do not concern matters of fact – they are about values. Our fundamental question is therefore one about the values necessary for group membership. Such values define a 'world view' which serves to guide thinking and doing within the group and also works to maintain and further the interests of the group.

It is now easy to see why the experience of teachers who undertake design courses is so valuable in exposing fundamental values within an ideology. As teachers, their conception of design contained a 'world view' with its own 'meaning-making' elements. It was to be expected that in relearning how to 'produce meaning' according to a diametrically opposed 'world view', teachers would experience contradictions in terms of their implicit position.

As we have already seen, the two aspects of the professionals' conception which proved difficult to assimilate within the teacher's 'world view' were concerned with 'range' and 'blank-slate' aspects. We now begin to look at these aspects in search of key values contained within. Both the 'range' and 'blank-slate' aspects led to a consideration of knowledge claims – a basic difference in belief here is concerned with the relative status of theoretic (scientific, design principles) and practical (derived from experience within given contexts) knowledge. We also found that the 'long-term' vs 'short-term' aspects of design were related to the separation of the design task from the implementation of a design.

Key or Core Values of the Professional Designer

It is the contention of this book that there are *two* key values of the professional designer. Both sub-groups (the curriculum expert and the educational technologist) adapt these values to suit their particular design activities. Indeed, each group asserts these values within its own tradition of historical development; also specialist terms and concepts are manufactured around these central values.

The two values are:

(1)   An insistence upon knowledge derived from 'rational' sources. Such a value might seem at first sight to be innocuous, yet behind it lies a belief in a particular view of rational knowledge and an attack upon skills and craft knowledge derived from the traditions of practice or intuitive means. It points to the use of theoretic knowledge as a means of legitimating control over the processes of teaching and learning.

(2) An insistence upon dividing the teaching/learning totality into a design phase and execution phase. Again, such a value appears almost common sense yet behind it lies a division of labour which can be used as a means of prevention of access to the totality of the teaching/learning situation. This value is a political necessity in establishing a group of educational designers who are to manage the teaching/learning situation.

The next two chapters are devoted to outlining the ways in which these two values are applied within the specific areas of design of educational technology and curriculum. Evidence of a specific adaptation of these values will be gathered from the professionals' 'world view' as depicted in courses of instruction, journals, handbooks, materials, development projects and the like. In this way each of the areas can be linked to these two central values. Thus, for each of the areas of design the specific 'world views' can be derived from the two central values. Indeed, these 'world views' are but adaptations of a management ideology as the two core values are essential for a group who wishes to manage others.

The Management Intent

To demonstrate how such values are used with management intent an analogy can be used. Suppose that a certain type of tree is growing in a garden. We may liken the tree to an idea structure which in effect defines the role of a teacher in institutionalised education. Expressed another way, the garden defines institutionalised education, while the tree stands for an ideology which supports and furthers the interests of teachers.

Now suppose that this tree is to be replaced by another. An axe to destroy the tree and a seed or sapling are required. The seed or sapling grows to become a new tree – in terms of our analogy, a new ideology has been established.

The axe of the analogy is provided by the first of the key values. The first value destroys the only basis upon which a knowledge claim by classroom practitioners can be made. A 'world view' of practical knowledge supposedly collapses under the rigor imposed by the competing and superior 'world view' provided by theoretic knowledge. The second value can be likened to the seed or sapling from which the management 'world view' is established.

Of course, it is well realised that this analogy is extremely simplistic – however, it may serve as a means to throw up other important questions such as: 'Was the original tree in a public garden?' 'Who wanted the change to a new tree – the gardeners or the public?' 'Who supplies axes and seeds?' But let us leave such questions for later.

The important point at this stage is that the two key values establish conditions in which control is outside of the reach of those who execute the action. That is, management of others is the intent behind such values. Indeed, this management intent is a central feature of each of the areas of curriculum and educational technology, and the way in which management manifests itself within each area is of considerable interest. In educational technology, for instance, there is strong feeling for 'classical' or scientific management styles related to the work of F. W. Taylor. This is not surprising, as Taylor's focus for management was production, and likewise the educational technologist derives managerial status from this avenue. Further, in modern-day terms Taylor's approach is described as the engineering or production approach; likewise we can identify a similar approach to production within educational technology.

In summary, our search for the meaning of the term educational design has eventually led us to align professional designers with managers – designers employ the key values of a management ideology to establish their control over the curriculum, materials production and evaluation. Each group has a 'working ideology' which, in terms of the values it employs, is a product of the management ideology. Often this management intent is disguised and covert – the emphasis upon technology for increasing the efficiency and effectiveness of an educational design leads to a concern with techniques rather than management as an issue.

Whether educational designers work with learning corporations or education systems, they seek to preserve or perhaps further their interests. To do otherwise would place them out of a job. It is to be expected then that designers foster and create a need for professionalised design products as part of their survival strategy. Consequently, professional designers have developed a number of interrelated arguments which support their quest for authority over the field of educational design.

This influence over the field of educational design does not stem from classroom practice – as teachers point out, professional designers do not trade in the natural authority which comes from participation on the classroom floor. Instead, authority and power are derived from 'management functions' and are transmitted through management values. For example, the label 'educational design' is denied to those skills, crafts and knowledge which are not integrated into the existing power structures within education. Educational design becomes a set of notions and skills that require formal processes of education for their transmission - for example, teacher training institutions offer specialist courses in educational design, and provide various diplomas which grant 'permission to practise' within this area.

Before we move on to a more detailed analysis of educational designers, a note about methodology may help.

Humanistic Sociology

Our approach has been sociological, but from a humanistic framework. That is, our intention is to investigate educational design and educational designers by attempting to describe 'world views'. In constructing such 'world views' we will attempt always to view things from the actors' perspective, recording how an object, person or situation is experienced and evaluated by those human agents who produced it and used it. Data, when considered this way, always belong to somebody or some group. This is a feature of humanistic sociology.

In organising data the 'meaning' attached to the object, person or situation by a group member is fundamental. Meanings are often structured in terms of core or fundamental values - that is, meanings are 'derived' from, and actions are guided by, the way that 'actors' use core values. There is an inherent circularity in defining either a social group or a set of core values - the social group is determined by its 'use' of the core values, and the core values are defined in terms of the way a group interprets and acts upon them.

In fact, core values are those which serve the stable operation of specific traditions which in turn help identify the social existence of particular groups. Thus, the core values already outlined serve to identify 'designers', and can themselves be identified through the interpretations and actions of those involved with educational design. Clearly, there are a number of derivative values which are a consequence of core values - these and the core values form an internally consistent set of values which define a 'world view'. Such 'world views' are ideological in that they serve 'meaning-making' and 'social-interest' functions for groups.

The analysis of the education 'culture' (or sub-culture) is therefore in terms of values. The contention of this book is that there are two competing value systems which are ideological in their functioning. So far we have outlined the core values of the 'professional designers' and, by implication, have suggested that the competing set of values belongs to 'teachers'. As yet we have not clearly delineated the core values of this group. This is quite intentional and the matter will be considered in later chapters.

However, for now, the main task is to show the action of the designers' core values in a number of areas. It is important to realise that job and role do not necessarily assign individuals to groups – for example, some teachers may well hold the core values of the professional designer and display a lack of commitment to 'teacher' values. This problem of describing and analysing the groups of the education sub-culture has been addressed by Wolcott (1977) who uses the anthropological concept of moieties. Broadly, a moiety is one of two mutually exclusive divisions of a group. He then applies the thesis that the educator sub-culture is distinguished by a moiety-like division that accommodates two divergent ideational sub-systems. The division is ever-present, but becomes apparent as a response to crisis situations. Wolcott continues by analysing educator moieties in terms of anthropological characteristics such as antithesis and rivalry, reciprocity, and complementarity.

While this analysis works from a similar viewpoint it does not attempt to outline social interactions between groups or claim a moiety division. Instead, it acknowledges the existence of at least two opposing 'world views' (called the professional designers' and teachers') which serve ideological functions.

The following two chapters are devoted to gathering detailed information about two areas of educational design in order to assess the extent to which educational design is a socially defined concept which serves group interests.

References

DETERLINE, W. A. 'Educational Systems', in *Technology and Innovation in Education: Putting Educational Technology to Work in America's Schools,* (Aerospace Education Foundation, Praeger, New York, 1968), p. 52

DISNEY, W. *Educational Media Catalogue,* (International Edition, 1977)

RICHMOND, K. *The Literature of Education – A Critical Bibliography 1945-1970,* (Methuen, London, 1972), p. 195

TAYLOR, F. W. *Principles of Scientific Management*, (Harper & Row, New York, 1947)

WOLCOTT, H. F. *Teachers Versus Technocrats: An Educational Innovation in Anthropological Perspective*, (Centre for Educational Policy and Management, University of Oregan, 1977), p. 242

4 EDUCATIONAL DESIGNERS: THE EDUCATIONAL TECHNOLOGIST

The previous chapter introduced the idea that the very notion of design and the existence of professional specialist groups involved with design requires the acceptance of two fundamental values. There are several features of these values: first, they serve to generate an ideology which belongs to educational designers and works to maintain and further their interests; secondly, these values are central to the existence of designers as a social group and so are strongly linked with 'identity' or role statements of educational designers; thirdly, and most importantly, the two values are strongly interactive and, in terms of the practical action they suggest, they can be taken together as a pair.

In considering each of these features of the values of the design ideology the specialist group of educational technologists will be considered first. Here the action of the ideological values is most evident, and, in addition, the orientation of educational technology has significant parallels with other design areas. In the field of curriculum we find that one conception, 'curriculum as technology', is almost identical with the position taken by educational technologists. Further parallels exist in the area of evaluation and critics point to the 'agricultural-botany' paradigm which has a number of striking similarities with the beliefs of educational technologists. In short, this conception of evaluation is systems oriented, and the metaphor characterises evaluation processes in terms of 'effective cultivation'. Plants as seedlings are weighed and measured, subjected to different conditions, and their growth and yields are statistically measured. Often control groups are used in order to assess the effects upon yield of changing a single factor within the growth conditions. Within this 'research' model of evaluation students are pre-tested, submitted to different educational designs, and their attainments measured by 'hard-data' approaches. The batch is statistically processed so that generalisations can be made about the effectiveness of the experiment (instruction).

To outline the ideological position of the educational technologist various sources will be used. In dealing with these we work from the position that the data contained within these sources are always 'somebody's', never 'nobody's' – that is, to interpret such information we seek to understand it in terms of how it functions in the experience of those who are actively dealing with it. Since our concern is to look at ideology as 'meaning-making' and 'social interest', the best sources for data are professional journals, texts and courses which induct students into the ways of 'meaning-making'. Consequently, the first two sources to be investigated are educational technology courses (and, in particular, educational technology courses within teacher training) and role and subject statements within professional literature.

The Concept of Educational Technology

What then is educational technology? For those teachers who are as yet unaware or untouched by the activities of educational technologists here is a list of some of the sorts of things that educational technology (and hence an educational technologist) is involved with:

(1) identifying characteristics, major practical problems and advantages of various teaching and learning strategies;

(2) identifying characteristics, practical problems and advantages of various forms of structured learning material;

(3) identifying characteristics, practical problems and advantages of various types of assessment procedures;

(4) identifying the technical characteristics of major forms of presentation media and their materials;

(5) identifying and writing long and short-term learning objectives in behavioural terms; checking their content validity;

(6) carrying out a content analysis of a topic and a course from defined objectives;

(7) identifying the influence of external factors affecting a specific situation;

(8) matching the characteristics of methods, materials and equipment to a specific situation;

(9) evaluating available materials, equipment and procedures for suitability in a specific situation;

(10) producing small units of structured learning;

(11) producing teaching materials for audio-visual presentation;

(12) devising and/or using simple retrieval systems to obtain access to existing resources;

(13) controlling and administering use of materials in learning situations;

(14) selecting or producing simple tests or assessment procedures for given situations;

(15) selecting and carrying out appropriate evaluation procedures in respect of (a) material, (b) results of a learning situation;

(16) interpreting evaluation data and using it to modify teaching and/or learning strategies and items of materials.

(City and Guilds, 1978)

The reason for quoting this list in detail is to give some idea of the scope of the self-appointed concerns of the educational technologist – it appears that there is little in the teaching/learning situation that the educational technologist considers himself not involved with.

Likewise, both the American and Australian 'definitions' express the global concerns of educational technology. For example, the AECT's (Association for Educational Communications and Technology) official definition and glossary of terms states that,

> educational technology influences who determines content, standardisation and choice of instruction, quantity and quality of instruction, who designs, produces and evaluates instruction, and who interacts with and assesses learners – and the effects of all this on the role of the teacher and the school system. (Silber, 1978)

Another way of describing this involvement is encapsulated in the definition adopted by the Australian Society for Educational Technology – here we find that educational technology is concerned with the 'design, application, evaluation, and development of systems, methods, and materials to improve the process of human learning.' It is interesting to note that the American statement is unashamedly political in that it is concerned with *who* determines how educational events should occur; however, it stops short of explicitly stating that educational technologists are in fact the effective managers, and instead is content to suggest that educational technology influences the decisions taken by some educational authority.

A further interesting role and domain statement is due to Silber (1970), who introduces the matter as follows.

> I guess the thing I dread most about cocktail parties is being introduced to Doctor Jones, Lawyer Smith, Accountant Black, Physicist Gordon or Psychiatrist Green, who, after they explain their jobs to me, ask the inevitable question, 'What field are you in?'

His answer is based around a model of instructional technology which is summarised as the development (research, design, production, evaluation, support-supply, utilisation) of instructional components (messages, men, materials, devices, techniques, settings), and the management of that development (organisation, personnel) in a systematic manner with the goal of solving instructional problems. In his 'search for identity' the paste which binds the multitude of 'components' together and defines a 'role' is the act of management. Expressed simply, educational designers supply organisation and personnel management to 'instructional development' for the purpose of control of 'instructional-system components'. It is interesting to note that the teacher is one such 'instructional-system component'.

Silber arrives at this conception of educational technology by making a number of what he calls 'big decisions' about the area of educational design – his first, and most important, being that he should not try to 'theoretically delimit' the scope of educational design by arbitrarily including some things and rejecting others. Instead, his task is to *'include them all'* (his emphasis), and to organise and manage all such factors!

Perhaps you are thinking that Silber's statement is a-typical and dated. After all, this sort of thing can be expected when considered against the buoyant educational scene of the late sixties. Surely, the educational technologist has come to see the realities of the seventies. Educational technology surely cannot include everything!

Well, perhaps educational technology does not mean the same as it did ten years ago, but to the likes of Kaufman (1978) the same emphasis on including everything is very much alive and well. In his recent role statement in *Educational Communication and Technology* he describes educational technology and educational technologists in the following way:

> Educational technologists have moved from a unique concern with the how-to-do-its of behaviour change (such as television, computers and instructional delivery systems) to the inclusion of *what* to teach. This expanded scope was encouraged and made possible by the pioneering work on measurable objectives.
>
> As soon as consideration of not only *how* and *what* were part of the technologists' repertoire, the inclusion of *why* was upon us. Tools and techniques, including needs assessment, needs analysis, system analysis and systems analysis, were all moving us not only toward a more efficient and effective job of changing (or maintaining)

behaviour, but also toward determining why something should be taught and why behaviour should be changed (or maintained) in the first place.

The formal consideration of *why* is a growing and thriving area of educational technology.

But perhaps the most popular exposition of the 'meaning' of educational technology is provided by Rowntree (1974) when he begins his book on educational technology in curriculum development thus,

> This book is not about audio-visual aids. My aim is not to promote television, teaching machines, computers and other teaching devices, ancient or modern. Educational technology is not to be confused with electronic gadgetry . . . educational technology is as wide as education itself: it is concerned with the design and evaluation of curricula and learning experiences and with the problems of implementing and renovating them. Essentially, it is a rational problem solving approach to education, a way of thinking sceptically and systematically about learning and teaching.

Historically, educational technology has arisen from a coalition of two movements. The audio-visual field was concerned to 'professionalise' itself and therefore required some theoretical self-justification – and, alongside of this, some psychologists and educationists, particularly those disposed towards programmed learning, saw the process of educational design as a 'second generation' programming movement which could apply systematic and scientific principles to education.

The early attempts at generating a 'science of instruction' were reflected in the definition initially used by the National Centre for Programmed Learning,

> Educational Technology is the application of scientific knowledge about learning, and the conditions of learning, to improve the effectiveness and efficiency of teaching and training. In the absence of scientifically established principles, educational technology implements techniques of empirical testing to improve learning situations. (Richmond, 1970)

Courses and Texts in Educational Technology

In the area of courses in educational technology we again find many interesting statements concerning subject and role. For example, in their Council for National Academic Awards Submission documents, an English polytechnic describes the situation thus,

> The Diploma (in educational technology) has its foundation in problem solving. The taught part of the course leads to a systematic approach to actual problems. Educational Technology is seen as the synthesis of existing areas of study and the application of the synthesis to problems in education and training. The technological approach parallels that of the structural engineer who brings together areas as diverse as metallurgy, geology and mathematics in the building of a bridge at a specified site. He focuses a range of competencies on a unique problem.
>
> We see the Diploma in Educational Technology as a synthesis of the range of competencies. We identify four major functions of the Educational Technologist and have therefore structured the course into four corresponding sections:
> 1. The analysis of learning needs and the design of strategies to meet these needs.
>   (LEARNING THEORIES AND APPLICATION);
> 2. The design and management of the learning environment most conducive to the meeting of those needs.
>   (ENVIRONMENT AND RESOURCES);
> 3. Curriculum analysis, development and design with reference to context, aims and structures.
>   (CURRICULAR APPROACHES);
> 4. The production of materials in a range of media to meet specified objectives.
>   (MEDIA).
>
> (Plymouth Polytechnic, 1979)

According to the information brochure of a Scottish college of education which deals with courses and consultancies in educational technology for curriculum development,

> Educational technology implies a shift from a predominantly intuitive attitude to teaching and learning towards a more systematic and analytic approach. The practical consequences of this change in

attitude include a closer attention to the definition of objectives, selection and systematic use of the most appropriate and effective techniques and devices, and attention to evaluation of results for the purpose of assessing or modifying the learning programme.

(Dundee College of Education, undated)

A Canadian university describes its Masters degree programme in educational technology in the following way,

The M.A. program is designed to prepare a new breed of educator, one who can identify educational needs and can apply new developments in psychology, in techniques of communication, in management theory or in systems analysis to solve them.

(Concordia University, undated)

In discussing the nature of the subject area, the same brochure contends that,

As an area of study and practice, educational technology spans several subjects. Its interdisciplinary nature becomes apparent when we realize that practitioners must consider radio and television not as broadcasters; computer-based systems not as computer scientists; learning problems neither as teachers nor psychologists; and planning for human resources development neither as economists nor as politicians. Educational Technology's invariant theme stresses the application of new scientific and technological developments to the solution of educational problems. It calls for professional competence in aspects of psychology, telecommunications, information systems, organisational science and engineering in addition to education.

Text books in educational technology emphasise similar sentiments but from the pragmatic viewpoint of defining good practice. For example, Gerlach and Ely's (1971) *Teaching and Media: A Systematic Approach* translates these concerns into the world of teaching. In their view behaviourism and systems are crucial to educational technology.

The basic premise behind the writing of this book is that media can be selected best and used most creatively when they are chosen on the basis of their potential for implementing specific objectives. Unless objectives are clearly defined first, selection of media is a chance matter. *Unless objectives are related to the larger concept of instructional design, they stand alone.* We are thus calling for a systematic design of instruction, with clearly stated objectives, and a selection of media based on their potential for implementing those objectives.   (my italics)

Many of the texts concern themselves with establishing the attitude that a technology of education is much more than the integration of techniques or methods with aids.

In order to establish a new viewpoint which differs from the old 'audio-visual aids' approach, texts in educational technology are careful to stress the difference between the two approaches. The basis of the difference is that educational technology is to be differentiated from the 'audio-visual aids attitude' in that the knowledge and processes of educational technology infuse into the curriculum process at a very early planning stage. Curriculum is depicted as a three-stage affair – curriculum determination, where the broad structures of the chosen content are outlined; curriculum planning, where this broad structure is transformed into objectives and the production of materials is carried out; and finally classroom implementation, where the materials and methodologies are implemented and assessed. Previously, audio-visual approaches were attached to the final stage of implementation, but now, in terms of the new framework of educational technology, the new techniques and knowledge (which subsume audio-visual approaches) become an essential part of the second vital stage. Indeed, so important is this phase of the curriculum process that its consequences extend into the two surrounding areas. In this sense educational technologists claim control over instruction and learning in the classroom through the application of knowledge and technique within the planning stage.

Another interesting area from which data concerning the 'world view' of the educational technologist can be gathered is that of the target populations of the various courses. Course members are drawn from specialist advisers to schools, colleges and industry, managers of resource centres or media services, and middle-management staff involved with curriculum development and materials production at departmental or institutional levels within the educational system. That is, the course provides 'management information' to a new breed of educational managers.

Educational Technology as Ideology

Now how does this 'world view' measure in terms of our ideological analysis of educational design? Are we able to clearly identify the two key values of the ideological position of the educational designer? And how are these key values applied within the practice of educational technology?

The first of the ideological values, which is concerned with an insistence upon knowledge derived from 'rational' sources, is clearly a feature of the educational technologists' position. Educational technology is not only the application of scientific knowledge about teaching and learning; in addition its techniques of application also embody the technological-rational approach. Indeed, as one of the statements contends, educational technology displays a movement towards systematic and analytic approaches. Thus the approach of the educational technologist is characterised by rational problem-solving.

As a professional in educational design the educational technologist approaches design problems with a special 'attitude' which contrasts sharply with what is called the 'traditional approach'. Significantly, this new attitude is linked with a different approach to the 'productive process'. As Chadwick (1973) notes, 'to provide the validated and co-ordinated educational materials (in the various media) required for optimal organisation and operation of the educational environment, the process of production of materials must also be significantly different.' Thus, a strong feature of such definitions or role statements is that they either state or infer that a certain attitude (i.e. a collection of values) is necessary if one is to be considered an 'educational technologist'.

The second ideological value was concerned with a division of the teaching and learning totality into a design and execution phase. That is, the conceptualisation of production for teaching and learning involves techniques which separate ends from means, design from execution, planning from implementation.

The influence of this value can be readily seen in the attempts of educational technologists to move their concerns towards the 'design' rather than the implementation end of curriculum development. The insistence that educational technology is not audio-visual aids is therefore a crucial catchcry for the educational technologist for, as we have already seen, to come too close to implementation is to make difficulties for claims made for theoretic knowledge. Clearly, this separation is related to the management intent, and consequently it is

not surprising to find that courses in educational technology are
directed towards management positions.

While these two ideological values can be seen in the role and
content statements of educational technology, this is not the prime
means of transmission for these values. Instead, the two values have
been translated into the content and methodological concerns primarily
through what is know as the 'systems approach'. What is extremely
interesting about this approach is its near unanimous, and largely
uncritical acceptance by educational technologists. We have already
touched upon the 'systems approach', and it is now time to extend
this initial contact.

The Systems Approach

So far the term systems approach has served as a broad label which
is linked both with a 'method' (scientific) and a way of 'viewing' a
problem. Educational technologists generally mix these two aspects –
indeed, to mix and not clearly differentiate is ideologically advantage-
ous. Actually, separate terms are often used (outside of educational
technology) to describe these two aspects.

A systems approach is basically a point of view, a way of looking
at things, a reconceptualisation based upon a management viewpoint.
Its distinguishing feature is scope – its desire to include all other
systems with which the system in question reacts. Its task is to describe
in broad strokes the interrelations and interreactions between systems.
Systems analysis is a methodology for examining a system. As a tool,
it sets out procedures by which a system is characterised – it enables
the outlining of functions, components, processes and interactions.
Thus systems analysis is a step in systems design and development.

Within educational technology there are about as many definitions
of the terms 'system', 'systems approach', and 'system and systems
analysis' as there are writers concerned with this area. About all that
can be said of the use of these terms is that the writers intend them as
'antonyms' of chaos. A system is conceived as a complex unity formed
from distinct parts which act independently and in interaction to
serve some purpose associated with the whole. Systems analysis
identifies the elements, determines the ways in which they work and
provides information on optimal functioning of the system. As we shall
later see, the educational technologist uses the term system approach
to include both 'reconceptualisation by wholes' and process (i.e. systems

analysis). In most instances the systems approach, as it applied within educational technology, is concerned with relatively small entities such as instruction or training, and its methodology is directed towards improving the efficiency and effectiveness of operation of this entity within the assumptions of broader systems. For example, if we use the terms systems approach and systems analysis as defined earlier, a systems approach to education would begin by outlining the inter-relations between the educational system and other interactive systems such as the social, political and economic. It would also mean describing the educational system in terms of its interactive sub-systems of primary and secondary schooling, higher education, and secondary schooling, vocational education, adult education and non-formal education. To carry this further would involve looking at elements of primary and secondary schooling from a systems viewpoint.

But this, of course, is not what educational technologists are concerned with! Their systems approach usually reconceptualises only the area in which they have some control over – this generally means that the approach merely serves the existing broad structures. As Hooper (1969) comments,

> educational technology ends up doing little else but perpetrating the traditional system of education. It is an abiding irony of the newer media that despite their ability to revolutionize and upgrade the quality of education, they can by the same token prolong and mirror what is already going on in school.

This observation is particularly relevant when we look at the way in which the 'systems approach' is used by educational technologists.

The systems approach as it is applied to teaching and learning serves to redefine the 'total' situation from the viewpoint of process – it is quite different from a traditional 'teacher-description' which works from content and the interpersonal relationships of the classroom.

Thus, a systematic analysis of the teaching and learning situation breaks this totality down into a number of component sub-systems such as content and objectives, pre-testing, physical facilities (space, time, resources, staff) and evaluation. These sub-systems are assumed to be relatively independent (a somewhat dubious assumption), so that changes in any of the sub-systems can produce a known 'tuning effect' on the system as a whole – that is, it is assumed that change in any one of the sub-systems can provide 'feedback' which allows further adjust-ments to be made to other sub-systems. For example, evaluation as a sub-system may (through testing based upon objective behavioural criteria) point to changes in either the level of pre-test or the initial objectives. The point is that this conception of the teaching and learning situation belongs to the educational technologist – and, as a technique it is directed towards control or management.

As a management technique it is directed at control of the classroom through control of a redefined totality. Once control over the totality is established it can be used as a means of prevention of access to the totality. Control within the teaching and learning situation requires an influence *outside* of the factors associated with implementation. This is due to the political realities of the teaching/learning situation – teaching is a highly personal activity which involves interpretation of ever-changing teaching and learning conditions. There is no real way that external controls can be placed upon the minute-to-minute changes within the classroom. But this does not mean that teaching and learning cannot be managed – while the classroom is not easily managed in any direct fashion, control can be asserted through larger issues such as the curriculum, materials production, and evaluation.

Consequently, while the minutiae of classroom teaching and learning are not amenable to direct control, they can be influenced by control over larger matters. In redefining the 'new' totality the educational technologist is demonstrating political control as this new 'world view' or 'construction of reality' ascribes control of the total to the educational technologist.

Thus, the systems approach is a way of thinking about the job of managing. Whether it be managing resources, managing resource production, managing design to control classroom events, or managing the people involved in the educational process, the systems 'technique' can be applied. In order that management is 'scientific' the systems approach brings with it the conviction that analysis and objectivity are key factors in the approach. The focus of the application of this approach within educational technology is *technique*. Many educationists attempt to portray the systems approach as a neutral technique borrowed from government, (especially the military) business and industry, which serves education in providing a rational approach to curriculum and materials production.

While the justificatory rhetoric for systems analysis is directed towards educational ends such as individualisation or resource-based learning, it would appear that educational technologists support this technique because it is a management procedure rather than any desire to reach such educational ends. This is evidenced by the frequency of insensitive and naïve statements concerning essentially political processes inherent in working towards such ends as individual-isation - in fact, it becomes increasingly difficult not to suspect that educational technologists are either a little dim-witted, or are so seduced by the promise of power and control through technique that they come to ignore (dare we say suppress^) the political implications of this technique.

Key (or Core) Values in Action

The systems approach serves both of the key values of the educational designer - it is both an attack upon the traditional and intuitive way of going about educational design and an instrument of means–ends separation. Let us see how this works with the case of a systems approach to *instruction*. Jerrold Kemp's (1977) *Instructional Design* gives one of the clearest and most inclusive statements on this matter.

> In order to intelligently relate all elements of the instructional process in building a successful program, an approach similar to one used widely in business, industry, the military and space exploration is receiving increased attention. This method involves the develop-ment of an overall plan incorporating the interrelated parts of an instructional process in a sequential pattern. It is called the systems approach to problem-solving. The process is based on the method of scientific inquiry, whereby a problem is recognized, a hypothesis is formed, experiments are conducted, and data are gathered from them that lead to a conclusion about the accuracy of the hypothesis. If it is correct, the results are used to produce or improve the products of technology. If not, new approaches are tried until success is realized.
>
> When this procedure is applied to instructional planning, the term instructional technology is used. It means the systematic design of instruction based on knowledge of the learning process and on communications theory, taking into consideration as many factors and variables of the particular situation as possible, so that success-ful learning will result . . .
>
> A method that focuses on learning outcomes, encompassing both the things we can specify and also those we can only anticipate, can become a realistic plan for designing improved instruction. It

can build on the old, making use of familiar language. It can draw from valuable experience in such areas as programmed instruction (specification matter in small steps, and continual evaluation of student learning) and techniques for producing audiovisual materials (primarily, production planning for motion pictures and television), and it can incorporate important elements from the systems approach.

First, let us consider the 'tone' of Kemp's statement. Presumably other approaches do not (or perhaps do so, but less effectively) intelligently relate *all* elements of instructional planning. We also note an inferred superiority of method through the association of the systems approach with the 'method of scientific inquiry'. Further, it is clear that Kemp expects a solution (or at least a limited number of solutions) to result which withstands empirical testing.

We further note that hypothesis formation rests with 'knowledge of the learning process [not teaching!] and communications *theory*'. Also, there is the hint that some factors and variables within the teaching and learning situation may be controlled or 'de-sensitised' so that successful learning will result. A *realistic* plan for *improved* instruction requires something more than the *old* 'approach'. And clearly the techniques of *product-production* planning (in this case television and motion-picture programmes) are important.

Considered as an ideological statement Kemp's characterisation is superb. It applies the first value by hinting that traditional knowledge and procedures are lacking, and require replacement with theoretic knowledge and scientific procedures. There is a clear dissociation from teaching – we note that Kemp's work is directed towards instructional rather than 'teaching' design. The second value of means–ends separation is covertly included within the statement. The producer–actor relationship is put forth in the television/motion-picture production-planning statement, while the emphasis upon the totality (i.e. 'intelligently relating all elements') suggests that someone other than the 'teacher-presenter' is involved.

Another 'classic' in terms of ideological implications is a metaphor provided by Luebbert (1972). The underlying military parentage of the systems approach come to the fore when, at an International Communications Symposium, he declared,

Let's consider a crude analogy. If we consider the classroom instructor as the 'academic artillery' with the academic equivalent of artillery forward observers, the academic equivalent of a fire-support coordination centre, and so on. Just as the organisation of the artillery can encompass such diverse weapons as mortars, howitzers, guns, rockets and guided missiles, why should not an academic support organisation include such diverse educational technology weapons [*sic*] as viewgraphs, slides, filmstrips, motion pictures, television and computer-assisted instruction? Forward observers become media consultants who work with individual academic departments, course directors and instructors to help them plan what kinds of media to use, when to use media, and when not to use media. A fire-support coordination centre becomes central location for coordination of all media requirements and capabilities to assure that television is not used where single-concept films would be more appropriate and effective, or to assure that a slide presentation is not used when overhead projection transparencies would be better.

This amazing characterisation of the teaching and learning process is the natural result of 'systems thinking'; the management ideology is, of course, vital to the 'chain of command' atmosphere of the armed services.

One of the real strengths of this ideological position is that it holds forth *process* as its visible and tangible trademark. Debate can therefore concern itself with the practical aspects of such processes leaving the matters of values and internal ideological position largely untouched.

Behaviourism

So far we have been concerned with the 'macro' aspect of educational technology - its reliance upon process through the systems approach. This broad structure is further strengthened through the application of the processes of behaviourism which account for the 'micro' structure of the subject. Indeed, the simultaneous application of the systems-approach and behavioural techniques are key factors in establishing educational technology. Cleary (1976), for example, considers that these areas represent identifiable traditions within educational technology.

A most interesting statement of this marriage of systems and behaviourism is given by Fraley and Vargas (1975) in an article directed towards university education entitled 'Academic Tradition and

Instructional Technology'. The ferocity of their attack upon academic tradition clearly exposes the basis of instructional technology. Sections from this article will be quoted in some length as they provide a stylistic and larger-than-life characterisation of the ideological position.

First we find that learning is defined in terms of behaviouristic criteria.

> Learning is change in behaviour and can be prescribed, produced, and guaranteed like any other product. It is now possible to specify the desired performance of learners and arrange the circumstances of learning such that those performances will be developed and exhibited by the learners. The behavioural products, explicitly delineated in advance, can and should be guaranteed. There is no theoretical reason why schools should produce ill-formed and inadequate behavioural products while we expect manufacturers of physical products to produce near perfect items.

By way of contrast we find that,

> There is an unfortunate trend in higher education, through a mix of ignorance and design, to avoid the objectivity of the newer behavioural and instructional technologies by obscuring the nature of the instructional process in a shroud of mystic elusiveness. Academicians propagate many ideas of that type: the goal of instruction is to impart truth and wisdom; instruction is a meeting of the minds; . . . By defining instruction in terms which defy translation to objective operational processes, the academic content expert can mitigate the organisation of criteria by which he might become excluded from his position of control.

So much for learning and objectives! The article then turns to systems. Here we find that,

> Instruction is a process, and the new organisational structure needed to accommodate our instructional missions must reflect the process itself.
>
> A complex process is accommodated by a system. Current popularity of the 'system approach' in educational jargon stems from an increasing awareness that instruction is a more complex process than traditionally assumed.

Well, so far so good. Now comes the managerial emphasis.

> The existing organisational structures in education will not support
> such rigorous and precise models of instruction, because traditional
> structures do not permit sufficient control over the many variables
> affecting instructional accomplishments. New structural arrange-
> ments are demanded which provide the expertise for this control.

Clearly, the issue is one of control and management. The authors
contend that it is time for a new 'academic' tradition to begin – a
tradition which is forged from their premises of behaviourism and
systems. In their view educational technology (or instructional technology) provides the leadership necessary to carry out revolutionary
changes.

So, for educational technologists behaviourism is an important
'aspect' of the systems approach – indeed, to consider it as separate
from systems puts it at the level of teaching methodology, where
behaviourism means specific lesson objectives and perhaps 'objective'
tests. Most conventional educational technologists are either behaviour-
ists or neo-behaviourists. To many, behaviourism in the form of
behavioural objectives provides the key to *applying* a systems approach.
On a pragmatic level the behavioural position provides definite prescriptive directives for going about educational design. The educational
technologist believes that a complex learning task can be broken up
into smaller tasks, and that the most useful unit for investigation of the
task, design of learning materials for achieving the task, selection of
media to assist the task, and evaluation of the resultant learning, is a
discrete overt behaviour. Behaviourism and effective educational design
therefore go hand in hand. Michael Macdonald-Ross (1972) summarises
this position as follows:

> It is claimed that behavioural objectives are completely sufficient
> for the purpose of prescribing the design of a learning system; for
> the purpose of prescribing the way in which the student's success
> may be evaluated; and as a public system of communication.
>
>   It is important to realize that these claims were meant in a strong
> sense. Design is so prescribed that only one, or a few, precise
> schedule(s) of reinforcement will lead to the terminal behaviour; one
> and only one, or a small isomorphic set of, terminal test(s) is
> consistent with the objectives; and the objectives show the learner
> unambiguously what his goals are, and also act as an unambiguous

public medium of communication between members of a design team.

For those teachers not fully conversant with the behaviourist position here are some of the more important assumptions behind the behavioural approach to educational design.

(1)   that, put simplistically, learning is change in behaviour;

(2)   that a complex behaviour can be broken down into a number of specific steps each with its own terminal behaviour;

(3)   that behaviours are accurate indicators of intents – i.e. if a student is able to state three facts about the geography of a region, that this behaviour is evidence supporting the 'interest', understanding or appreciating the geography of a region. Or, to put it another way, the objective and the terminal behaviour are considered isomorphic;

(4)   that the different kinds of learning can be usefully analysed in terms of cognitive, psychomotor and affective categories. Cognitive and affective learning can only be reliably established when an observable behaviour is designated or associated with a particular learning task in these areas;

(5)   that, ideally, a well stated behavioural objective answers four questions which relate to the 'point of departure' of an educational journey. The journey analogy, which will be used again later is often cited as providing a disarmingly simple reason for the priority of objectives. Briefly, the objectives position is framed in terms of the statement that 'to know whether one has arrived at a destination, one must first know the destination'. The analogy is used further as there is also the belief that after one knows the destination the means (both the pathway and the type of vehicle) for reaching it will become apparent. The four 'point of journey' questions asked of the destination are:

(i)   Who? The answer must be stated in terms of the learner.
(ii)   What? The destination must be terminal in some sense and be stated in terms of observable behaviours.
(iii)   When? Under what particular conditions is such a journey to be undertaken.
(iv)   How well? If we don't reach the stars will the moon do?

(6)   that once such explicit objectives are set the problems of assessment of learning are reduced;

(7)   that the selection of the means to achieve such objectives

is consequent upon pre-planning the objectives. The sequencing of learning (tasks and content) designed to achieve such objectives parallels the logical hierarchy of objectives;

(8) that by using behavioural objectives a common language might be established to facilitate communication between the curriculum planners who determine the curriculum, the educational technologist who implements it by materials production, the curriculum evaluator and the teacher.

These eight 'assumptions' provide 'ways of acting and thinking' within the broad sub-systems of the instructional system. For example, the systems approach to instructional design which employs behaviourism has ready made answers about stating objectives, content organisation and sequencing, media selection and evaluation. Thus, this approach applies an empirical, internally self-consistent 'logic' for educational design. The importance of this 'logic' cannot be stressed too strongly – the union of behaviourism and systems within the area of instructional design provides one of the simplest and most compelling accounts of how educational design *should* be practised. The fact that such approaches may not accurately describe current realities in the way teachers practise design is unimportant. The approach does not describe, it prescribes an ideal!

Training Systems

One area in which this sort of 'logic' is allowed almost total control is in the development of *training* systems. The Royal Australian Navy School's *Training Systems Manual* (1976), for example, describes the 'simple and effective' principles of training technology in the following way:

> Training objectives must be job derived; the successful design of training courses emanates from careful *analysis* of what the job requires. This analysis leads to preparation of *training objectives* and *performance tests*, followed by the design of a course to produce the required performance. In the design phase consideration must be given to *methods and media* that best achieve the objectives. Instruction is then conducted and learning tested. Feedback is derived by *evaluation* of the processes performed in the training school and *validation* of on-the-job performance to see

whether the training system is effective. Information obtained in this *quality control* process may then be used to modify any or all of the sub-systems which comprise the complete training process. In this way training can be updated and improved.

The training-technology system is administered by a training administration which has two 'clear administrative' tasks - course implementation and administrative support. That is, the instructor-trainee interaction must be managed by 'designers' who control the areas of management of instructional staff, training development, syllabus design and modification, administration of tests, course planning and scheduling.

So, within a training technology such as this the instructor (teacher?) is very definitely a part of a systems approach which is managed by an administration. The two key values of the design ideology are unashamedly in the service of tight 'line management' in which power for decision-making is highly centralised. The implementer (instructor) receives and executes orders from above. The strong 'rational' design approach extends to techniques of 'network schedules', objective training-statement schedules, module-specification guides and the like. And the insistence upon dividing the teaching and learning totality into a design and execution phase is a feature of the training-task analysis.

What is important about such a training technology is that it is conceived as a *technology* - that is, as a technique in which the principles behind the technology can be applied to similar tasks. After all, what is technology if it is not the science of *application of knowledge* to practical purposes. Consequently, adaptations of this technique appear in teacher training or any training task. For example, a paper presented at the International Association for Programmed Learning and Educational Technology conference in 1979 deals with 'a modular system of self instruction in educational technology within a course of teacher training'. In its design 'self-instructional modules incorporating flow-charts, algorithms and the management technique of network analysis were compiled based upon a systematic analysis of the learning process and including specific objectives for the tasks involved.' (Wood, 1979). Another example of a general training system is supplied by Hudson's (1979) 'Sheffield System'. The number of variations of this 'technology' are virtually endless.

Control over the Hardware of Materials Production

So far we have considered data from which we have outlined the 'world view' of the educational technologist. We have shown that this 'conception of reality' depends upon two key values, and that the ideology of the educational technologist employs these values within the systems approach and behaviourism. Examples of the systems approach applied to instruction and training have provided evidence of the action of the ideological values held by educational technologists.

But before moving on to design as practised by the curriculum leader, one further aspect of educational technology needs to be considered. This is the special claim made by educational technologists for control over the instruments of educational materials production. The educational technologist trades in knowledge of 'instruments' such as video-systems, photographic and audio machines, overhead and slide projection equipment, 16-mm film, reprographic equipment and a host of other devices. And as we have already mentioned, educational technology owes its very existence, in part, to the influx of equipment into educational systems.

The American situation provides the clearest example of this equipment-based development. The notion of educational design became important when government and military training programmes in World War II were forced to rely upon 'communications media' due to a lack of qualified instructors. Such programmes provided 'the most important impetus' for the design of media-based (primarily in film) mass-training schedules (Hitchens, 1979). With the ending of hostilities the time was ripe to apply such techniques to mass education.

The next significant boom period, which was to last for near twenty years (1958-73), was initiated by the passing of the National Defense Education Act (1958). This Act provided vast funds which were to revolutionise the American audio-visual education movement. The effect of this new push can be seem in terms of the response of the academic system. American doctoral dissertations in the audio-visual/ media area in the period (approx.) 1936-56 seem to be concerned with cost-effectiveness and the viability of applying audio-visual procedures to general education. As Moldstad (1956) points out, 'two thirds of these studies were specifically concerned with audio-visual media and with experimental evaluations of their effectiveness' and 'far too few . . . designed to test the effectiveness of audio-visual materials in various academic areas and in particular levels within various disciplines.' The concern was for an overall feasibility study which supported the 'equipment-based' group of educationists. The new boom brought research projects and professionals from communications – the new 'breed' of the sixties redefined audio-visual education in terms of professional 'areas' taken from communication theory and psychology. Studies now became media-specific, and concerned with the way that media properties influence learning.

However, the hope that research-based 'theoretical knowledge' would provide a rationale for this emerging group was not realised. Comparison studies which attempted to provide evidence of the superiority of media and equipment-based teaching and learning did not clearly indicate any significant differences (statistically) between different media or media and conventional approaches. Indeed, it took some fifty years of 'media research' before educational technologists were to admit that,

> despite reports from earlier evaluative studies, however, we have no solid experimental proof that the use of non-verbal media solely because there are such media will lead automatically and universally to greater learning than the use of non-media forms of instruction.
> (Allen, 1973)

To be specific, in the area of television Saettler (1968) comments that,

> Stickell (1963) analyzed some 250 media comparison studies of televised instruction and direct instruction and classified 217 as 'uninterpretable', 23 as only partially interpretable because of defects in experimental design, and only 10 studies as interpretable. All of these 10 showed no significant differences in learning at the .05 level between televised and direct instruction.

Such research findings pose difficulties for a 'media-based' educational technology – consequently the 'nuts and bolts aspect', that is the equipment or hardware side of the movement, was played down. Instead, as we have already seen, 'technology' becomes associated with techniques rather than equipment.

It is quite important to realise that this emphasis upon 'technique' rather than 'nuts and bolts' is for ideological reasons. In reality the educational technologist must be concerned with devices and equipment, as it is this fact which distinguishes him/her from the curriculum leader or evaluation expert. There is a considerable dilemma here – to 'professionalise' the area it must be seen to be more than equipment yet to establish 'boundaries' with other subjects this equipment aspect is central. Without control over the instruments of production the educational technologist loses much of his/her 'public' identity. The core values central to this identity have been established through an involvement with design through control over the instruments of production - without this design function the educational technologist comes to be cast as an equipment-using technician serving a 'designer'.

Thus, the educational technologist has continued to maintain control over audio-visual 'services' such as equipment purchase and maintenance in order to demonstrate management of this area. The lack of a research-based justification has not hampered the management role - research is but one factor considered in the practical task of management.

Power Structures and Educational Technology

As middle management, educational technologists have been obliged to work within the existing and 'traditional' power structures of education. Travers, (1973) in the *Second Handbook of Research in Teaching* is one of the few writers who have considered educational technology and related research in terms of its role within 'power structures'. The twin features of his analysis are that, first,

> Technology, when its development is sponsored by a government or by the group in power, tends to develop only those ideas and devices that are of particular value to the government or power group. Technology developed under these conditions is likely to be reactionary and far removed from the welfare of the people. Indeed, it is likely to be detrimental to the people, for it has commonly been used to maintain the power of a particular government or power group.

and secondly that,

> One of the interesting features of operant psychology is that it can be described to an extraordinary degree by a statement of the assumptions that underlie the workings of modern capitalistic socety . . . Both operant psychologists and influential sources of power in the American culture seek new techniques of exerting improved control over human behaviour.

His analysis continues by pointing out that educational technology is intensely conservative, and is essentially an instrument which preserves the *status quo* of the establishment.

It is not that other educationists have not noted this conservatism – indeed, they point out that there is something quite incongruous about the educational technologists own role statements and the actual involvement in the wide-ranging management decisions that a systems approach might suggest. In such circumstances the educational technologist is careful to retain control over production media and hardware, as they represent the one clear area that existing power structures in education have delegated.

In serving this conservative role educational technologists realise full well that their existence depends upon equipment control and definitions of the field which stress process. Equipment provides the avenue towards design, and process definitions give rise to a concern for instructional development and not merely for a particular communications medium or resource. Instructional development is larger than product (or materials development), and incorporates a whole range of design activities. Management and design go hand in hand.

In this chapter we have seen the way in which the core values of a management position have been transformed into an ideology which serves educational technologists. The notions of systems and behaviourism are central to this belief system. The next chapter examines another area of educational design – that of curriculum design.

References

ALLEN, W. H. 'What Do 50 Years of Media Research Tell Us?' *Audio Visual Instruction*, (March, 1973), pp. 48-50

CHADWICK, C. 'Educational Technology: Process, Prospects and Comparisons', *British Journal of Educational Technology*, vol. 2, no. 4, (1973), pp. 80-94

City and Guilds. *Syllabus Pamphlet T/731*, (London, 1978)

CLEARY, A., MAYES, T. and PACKHAM, D. *Educational Technology*, (Wiley, London, 1976)

Concordia University. *Graduate Studies in Educational Technology*, (undated brochure)

Dundee College of Education, *Courses in Educational Technology*, (undated brochure)

FRALEY, L. E. and VARGAS, E. A. 'Academic Tradition and Instructional Technology', *The Journal of Higher Education*, vol. XLVI, no. 1, (1975), pp. 1-16

GERLACH, V. S. and ELY, D. P. *Teaching and Media: A Systematic Approach*, (Prentice Hall, New Jersey, 1971), p. 2

HITCHENS, H. 'The Evolution of Audio Visual Education in the U.S.A. since

1945', *Educational Media International*, no. 3, (1979), pp. 6-12

HOOPER, R. A. 'A Diagnosis of Failure', *Audio Visual Communication Review*, vol. 17, no. 3, (1969), pp. 245-71

HUDSON, E. *The Sheffield System*, (Paper available at APLET 79, 1979)

KAUFMAN, R. 'From How to What and Why: The Search for Educational Utility', *Educational Communication and Technology*, vol. 26, no. 2, (1978), p. 118

KEMP, J. *Instructional Design*, (Fearon, California, 1977), p. 6

LEUBBERT, W. F. 'Instructional Technology, Education and Man as a Builder and User of Tools', International Symposium on Communication: Technology, Impact and Policy, The Annenberg School of Communications, University of Pennsylvania, March 23-25, 1972. Quoted in Schiller, H. I., *The Mind Managers*, (Beacon, Boston, 1973), p. 78

MACDONALD-ROSS, M. 'Behavioural Objectives and the Structure of Knowledge', in Austwick, K. and Harris, N.D.C. (eds), *Aspects of Educational Technology VI*, (Pitman, London, 1972), pp. 38-47

MOLDSTAD, J. 'Doctoral Dissertations in Audio-Visual Education', *Audio-Visual Communication Review*, vol. IV, no. 4, (1956), pp. 291-333

Plymouth Polytechnic. *CNAA Diploma in Educational Technology*, (1979), p. 10

RICHMOND, W. K. *The Concept of Educational Technology*, (Weidenfeld & Nicolson, London, 1970), p. 5

ROWNTREE, D. *Educational Technology in Curriculum Development*, (Harper and Row, London, 1974), p. 1

Royal Australian Navy. *Training System Manual*, vol. I, Introduction, (1976), p. 3

SAETTLER, P. 'Design and Selection Factors', *Review of Educational Research*, vol. XXXVIII, no. 2, (1968), pp. 115-27

SILBER, K. H. 'What Field Are We In, Anyhow?' *Audiovisual Instruction*, (May, 1970), pp. 21-4

SILBER, K. H. 'Problems and Needed Directions in the Profession of Educational Technology', *Educational Communication and Technology*, vol. 26, no. 2, (1978), p. 177

TRAVERS, R. M. 'Educational Technology and Related Research Viewed as a Political Force', in Travers, R. M. (ed), *Second Handbook of Research on Teaching*, (American Educational Research Association, Rand McNally, Chicago, 1973), pp. 979-96

WOOD, A. 'A Modular System of Self Instruction in Educational Technology within a Course of Teacher Training', paper presented at APLET conference (1979)

5 EDUCATIONAL DESIGNERS: THE CURRICULUM LEADER

When considering the educational technologist as an educational designer, comment was made about the degree of overlap in role and function between curriculum leaders and educational technologists. This similarity could be taken as an indication that the two 'types' of educational designer could well be considered as the one and same player of the 'game' of educational design. However, our stance has been to view areas of educational design from the actor's perspective, and since each of the designers engage in 'boundary maintenance' (they are concerned with questions of their identity and subject concern), we therefore consider each of the designers as they consider themselves – that is, as separate, identifiable professionals involved with management through design. The relationship between the two groups can be seen through the professional literature of each of the fields.

The Curriculum Leader and the Educational Technologist

Curriculum leaders carry out subject-boundary maintenance in a particularly effective fashion – their literature simply does not acknowledge the 'professional' status of the educational technologist. There is an extraordinary lack of communication between educational technologists and curriculum leaders and, in broad terms, each ignore each other's writings. Wilkes (1978), for example, carried out a small-scale survey directed at finding out whether the two groups of practitioners cite or write for each other. His general conclusions were that 'curriculum theorists do not read the works of educational technologists' and that if 'curriculum theorists may rightly be accused of not reading educational technology, then some more space must be found in the dock for educational technologists themselves.'

This situation is all the more astounding when we consider the overlap between the fields. James (1978) summarises courses in educational technology and curriculum with regard to role statements and content and comments that,

Generally, the roles stated in relation to curriculum development are broader and appear to subsume the more specific statements provided in relation to the educational technology field. At the same time, however, the role statements within the educational technology field seem to refer to 'curriculum development' as a subset of its own activities. So each field gives some indication of claiming to contain the other.

Despite such claims he ventures the opinion that 'the curriculum-development field may be seen to have a broad managerial focus while the educational technology field has a narrower focus on the practical and design problems involved.' The basis of this position is the claim that the main differences between educational technology and curriculum are the central place of social and philosophical issues within curriculum (educational technology avoids such matters) and the highlighting of media selection, resource use and productional techniques by educational technology (curriculum avoids productional techniques).

But this issue of 'focus' is very much a matter of opinion. The curriculum leader and the educational technologist are often attempting to manage the same broad area of educational change. Indeed, a role statement of the curriculum leader provided by the Association for Supervision and Curriculum Development parallels that of the educational technologist: in their view, the curriculum leader 'is to provide leadership and management expertise essential to planning, developing, implementing and evaluating the curriculum.' (Bartoo, 1976). This compares with the statement concerning educational technology as the design, application, evaluation and development of systems, methods and materials to improve the process of human learning.

This overlap in role and function is further reflected in the so called 'definitions' of curriculum. According to an Australian report on a Curriculum Development Centre National Workshop,

The term 'curriculum' is open to a number of interpretations, broad and narrow. Under the broad definition, curriculum is 'what happens in school to influence the development of children', and thus includes not only what children study, but the way in which it is presented and the very organisation of the groups in which they study, as well as the form of the class/teacher interaction.

The report continues by stating that,

Nested in this broad definition are more narrow concerns such as the outline of a particular sequence of topics or skills in a particular subject area (the 'syllabus') and printed and other audio-visual materials and suggested activities which a teacher and her students might use.

A somewhat narrow view of curriculum development sees it as resulting in just these kinds of materials and activities, together, perhaps, with suggested sequence, activities and methods of presentation.

(Curriculum Development Centre, 1974)

The 'narrow view' is often process oriented. English and Kaufman (1975), for example, put this position,

Curriculum is a means to an end. It is the conscious and deliberate shaping of the major elements at the disposal of the educator to reach validated student objectives. These elements represent assumptions about time, space, learning and teaching, and the relationships between teacher and students brought together within varying types of schedules to reach those objectives of which the curriculum stands as the composite configuration. As such the curriculum is the final process tool to be used to reach such objectives and it is subject to a complex set of assumptions and decisions.

So the curriculum leader, like the educational technologist, claims wide (and often exclusive) influence over educational design. Both groups see their 'role and function statements' as evidence for such claims.

The interpretation of the relationship between these two areas in relation to their management function shows wide variation – from each viewing the other as subservient to a reciprocating interdependence. Where the management ideology strongly infuses the conception of curriculum (and hence curriculum design), we find the notion that educational technology is a narrow speciality which serves the technical needs of a phase of curriculum – that of curriculum development. Thus, within a curriculum project one would expect a curriculum-oriented project manager handing down the technical requirements of his team to the educational technologist who might be regarded as a 'technician'. On the other hand, the reverse of this relationship occurs where educational technologists view the function of the curriculum expert as limited to the provision of a series of broad working educational goals – from this point onwards the educational technologist, as an expert developer, materials producer, evaluator, innovation strategist, and resource manager takes over. Curriculum development and implementation are thus part of the educational technologist's role!

Let us leave the matter of role competition between educational technologists and curriculum planners for the moment, and investigate further role and subject statements provided by curriculum designers.

One thing appears clear when we investigate the area of curriculum design - more controversy exists within the field of curriculum over matters concerning curriculum design than anything else. This is not surprising, as curriculum design is virtually the focal point of all curriculum thinking. And as we have already hinted, this centrality is due to the fact that it is through 'design' that management by curriculum experts occurs.

Curriculum Leaders and Curriculum Workers

The fact that curriculum presents such a broad front and inevitably involves a wide range of educationists is somewhat of a problem for professional educational designers. Clearly, such a situation is unstructured and largely unmanageable. Consequently, if the curriculum designer is to exert a managerial influence a division of labour must be established. Thus, the most fundamental role distinction within the area is between the 'curriculum worker' and 'curriculum leader'. Consequently, we find the Association for Supervision and Curriculum Development stating that,

> The term 'curriculum worker' applied to most educators - whether central office administrator, teacher, or principal. The term 'curriculum leader' applied to that person with primary responsibility for the planning, co-ordination, and/or management of curriculum activity in a district.
>
> (Speiker, 1976)

Not surprisingly, curriculum *workers* are 'implementers', while curriculum leaders are concerned with design.

The question of who should have control over curriculum design is a continual problem within the field of curriculum. The existence of this problem is an unavoidable consequence of a 'model' of curriculum design - a model which, according to Inglis (1974), is a direct product of modern technocracies. As a style of thought which dominates curricular and educational planning, it

> appeals to a model of reason whose terms derive from the coarse
> utilitarianism developed for the administration of social welfare in
> a mass competitive and consumer society. This model defines
> practical objectives and aims to calculate probable human responses
> to them. Such models cannot . . . answer tests of rationality, but
> pass themselves off as rational because they answer the criteria of
> cost, productivity, growth and efficiency as defined by the input-
> output economists . . . In the absence of opposition, these criteria
> now provide the instructional models for the control and evalua-
> tion of public knowledge.

That is, the 'style of thought' behind many curriculum-design models is
directly related to management of learning. In fact, the 'teacher-proof'
curriculum is a classic example of how a designer might manage the
teaching and learning situation by 'by-passing' the teacher. Thus curriculum design as an issue continually poses the question of who controls
design. Further, this question has no single or standard answer – control
over school-based curriculum development poses different concerns
from control over a national curriculum project.

Curriculum Design and the Teacher

Whatever the context within which curriculum design is carried out,
decisions about the teacher's role in curriculum design must eventually
be made. Beauchamp (1975) puts the issue this way.

> To think of involving teachers additionally in anything as compli-
> cated as a curriculum system (as it has been described in the
> preceding pages) appears to be impossible. It is impossible unless
> ways and means for teachers to participate are found, and the
> principal ingredient in the ways and means is time unencumbered
> by teaching responsibility for work on curriculum tasks. Conse-
> quently, the two big questions about this choice of involvement
> are whether one believes that classroom teachers should be involved
> in curriculum engineering and whether one is willing to develop the
> ways and means for doing so, assuming the answer to the first
> question is in the affirmative.

The concept of school-based curriculum development brings the issue of control over design into sharp focus. The value position of school-based curriculum development is clear: of all educational agencies, bodies and institutions it is the school and school teacher which should have the primary responsibility for determining the content of the curriculum, the learning resources and methodologies necessary for teaching and learning and the evaluative techniques. Control and management is therefore at the school level and often invested in a middle-management position within the school – the deputy or assistant headteacher often fulfils this role. Control over the classroom is merely a little more immediate!

While actual control becomes invested in middle management, it is interesting to note that writings concerned with school-based curriculum development often stress the egalitarian nature of this movement. For example, a submission for accreditation for Post Graduate Studies in Curriculum Development from an Australian college of advanced education notes that the literature in the area of school-based curriculum development is significant in that it is, 'not simply . . . (a) salutary stress on new responsibilities and increasing professional expertise for teachers but also . . . (is) directed not to a professional elite but to the broad spectrum of teachers.' (Northern Rivers CAE, 1979)

But what would happen if 'the broad spectrum of teachers' were actually able to carry out curriculum development within a school? Suppose that teachers did have the necessary time for such activities, and had received the theoretical basis and technical design skills from a course which emphasised school-based-curriculum development. Under such conditions individual teachers might well produce their own curriculum documents for their subject areas – the inbuilt assumptions and values behind a syllabus would reflect an individual's beliefs about such things as the function of schooling, the political system, the importance of their subject area, the relationship between work and leisure and a host of related matters. In other words, a legitimate curriculum document could attempt a 'reconstruction' of values (social, political, ethical, economic, to name but a few) towards an ideal held to be important by the teacher. It would be quite probable that a second teacher in the same subject area might produce a radically different curriculum based on an alternative set of values! For example, two science teachers might produce radically different curricula based upon their interpretations of such things as the role of science in society, its relationship with technology and the status of scientific knowledge.

Consequently, a possible outcome of school-based curriculum development is a situation where there is a lack of consensus about value matters – the school could therefore have no identifiable policy about their approach to schooling (perhaps, except that they intend to have none) and the subject areas will also lack agreement over their general goals and aims.

Now such a situation (which tends towards teacher-based rather than school-based curriculum development) is a denial of the notion of curriculum in its macro sense. Marklund (1974), from the Swedish National Board of Education, for example, points to this problem in the following way:

> To me it is a big question, if the term curriculum is at all useful and meaningful, unless one presumes a certain organisational and administrative structure of the school, a form of organisation and administration in which the individual school works as a clearly defined unit.

Such fragmentation at the level of the individual teacher undermines much of what a 'systems-oriented' concept of curriculum design is all about. As we have already noted, professional educational design implies prescription, and curriculum design, in particular, is aimed at providing control and lines of authority over larger issues such as the subject development within a school or school district, the balance between various subjects in each grade level and the like.

So, in the last analysis, school-based curriculum development cannot be cast in this egalitarian fashion. It too is directed towards middle management (though in a local or regional sense), and is therefore concerned with exerting control over the classroom floor.

Curriculum Design as Ideology

Having acknowledged the diversity of situations to which 'curriculum design' is relevant, it is now time for us to investigate curriculum design as ideology – that is, our concern will be to look at the 'meaning-making' and 'social-interest' aspects of design from sources such as professional journals, texts and courses. As with our analysis of educational technology, we will be interested in tracing the influence of the two central values associated with educational design within the area of curriculum.

One of the most obvious movements in the area of curriculum (at least in terms of the American literature) is the stress on 'scientific curriculum-making'. As Kliebard (1975) puts it,

> it should be clear to anyone familiar with the current state of the art in the curriculum world that the scientific curriculum movement, with few adaptations and modifications, has been triumphant . . . While this modern version of scientific curriculum making is well established in virtually all sectors of the curriculum world, it exists, not surprisingly, in its most virulent form in the area of teacher education.

In the absence of any overarching 'theory' about curriculum this scientific mode was assisted by the application of other theoretic knowledge from disciplines in the social sciences. Such applied knowledge, derived from scientific sources, is put forth as 'principles' of design. This dependence on the theoretic knowledge of other areas is described by Pinar (1978): 'The view that education is not a discipline in itself but an area to be studied by the disciplines is evident in the work of those curricularists I have called conceptual-empiricists.'

Curriculum design is therefore conceived as a 'scientific undertaking' which applies an amalgam of discipline studies to its service. This 'scientific' influence has spawned an approach to curriculum in which the 'atom' is termed a curriculum 'unit'. That is, curriculum units or teaching/learning units could be designed by reference to 'principles' of learning and instruction. The commonly identified steps for the design process were: diagnosing needs, formulating specific objectives, selecting content, organising content, selecting and organising learning experiences, evaluating and checking for balance and sequence. The curriculum therefore emerges from 'design' issues summarised by catch cries such as the MPIR approach (motivation, plan, implementation, review) NOSE (needs, objectives, strategies, evaluation) or the like. Such approaches are obviously 'systems' oriented in much the same way that educational technologists approach design.

While such approaches are part of the American scene, there is the feeling among commentators on curriculum development that, 'In some countries, of course, there have been strong traditions of teacher independence in curriculum building. Britain stands out, particularly the extensive primary school reforms effected in the United Kingdom since the end of World War II.' (Centre for Educational Research and Innovation, 1975). However, as Michael Young (1976) notes of the Schools Council in the United Kingdom,

Up till 1973, 91 out of 125 projects were located in universities, and only three in schools, which would seem to indicate an unquestioned assumption that curriculum development *for* schools is best located outside them (in universities) – thus institutionalizing the separation of theory from practice.

He also points out that individual teachers in the classroom may be able to choose resources and in general gain the impression that they have considerable autonomy – however, he reports that when a *group* of teachers tried to influence decisions relating to such classroom matters difficulties were experienced. Thus, 'in making the elements of constraint less obvious to practising teachers this apparent autonomy actually obscures its reality and therefore any possibilities of change.' Consequently, the politics of control in the area of curriculum design would appear relevant to the differing situations of both the United Kingdom and the United States.

Core Values – The Interpretation by Curriculum Leaders

Already we can discern the influence of the two key values in the area of curriculum design. While it is evident that their influence is attenuated by the wider and more diverse concerns of curriculum, it is there, nevertheless. Our two key values were:

(1)   An insistence upon knowledge derived from 'rational' sources. Scientific 'principles' and theoretic knowledge are held more reliable than craft knowledge derived from the traditions of practice or intuitive means.

(2)   An insistence of dividing the teaching/learning totality into a design-and-execution phase. A redefined totality emerges in which control is invested in the educational designers.

The first value appears through the emphasis upon curriculum *theory* and the resultant models of the curriculum process. In terms of our previous analysis of educational technology the 'curriculum model' is akin to a systems outline!

The distinction between systematic and systems is again relevant in the area of curriculum development. In general terms a broad distinction can be drawn between system-based curriculum development and subject-based curriculum development (which might also be put in terms of a systematic approach). The literature of curriculum develop-ment, like that of educational technology, often blends the terms system and systematic to a common meaning.

The 'scientific' (called systematic or systems) approach to curriculum-making contrasts with what is often disparagingly referred to the *ad hoc* curriculum or traditional model. One suspects that this 'approach' has been termed a 'model' merely to add to the intended contrast between scientific-theoretic based models of curriculum! Design carried out within the 'traditional model' is subject-matter dominated, methods oriented, and suffers from unclear aims and philosophy, inappropriate logic for sequencing and narrow evaluation. Little heed is paid to such theoretic concerns as psychological factors, learning theories, the philosophy of knowledge, instructional media, evaluative techniques and so on. The implication seems to be that without a firm theoretic-prescriptive base, teachers carry out or implement design in a haphazard and *ad hoc* way. The result is an unsatisfactory 'evolutionary' process which arrives at a course which, at best, is typified as the transmission of a loose jumble of 'pearls of wisdom' by ineffective teachers!

The 'scientific' alternatives, of which there are many, all reject this approach. The means-end or product model, which is an example of subject-based systematic course development, is one approach which blends theoretic knowledge into a scientifically based way of curri-culum design. As we have already discussed this approach when con-sidering unit design, little more needs be said.

Research and development models likewise often tend towards 'scientism' – that is, their approach is rooted in attempts at simulating 'scientific method' within the educational context. Experts delineate a problem and apply a research, development and diffusion strategy. However, such models depend upon two assumptions – first, acceptance of the solution to the problem is by 'rational' means, and secondly, that the solution can be applied by any teacher. Indeed, such models largely remove themselves from the real world of classroom practice, and are content to assume that acceptance of these two assumptions is a matter of 're-educating' teachers into this research-and-development 'world view'. Any intransigence displayed by teachers merely confirms the educational designers outlook that teachers are basically inadequate in the area of design due to their inability to grasp such new approaches.

Under such a 'model' teachers are ready to point out that their participation as researchers and developers is usually limited to superficial involvement. As Harlen (1977) states,

Most of the projects in the Schools Council's early programme 1967-72 and the Nuffield Science Projects involved teachers in this way (weak research and weak development role), even if it was not the only kind of teacher participation practised. These projects tended to follow a fairly clear pattern of initial investigation, production of materials, trials and evaluation, followed by publication. Involvement of teachers at the trials stage typically required them to use specified materials in specified ways and during a specified time interval. Feedback from trials included teachers' opinions of the drafts, which were used to make revisions, usually only minor, in content or presentation of teaching materials but not more fundamental changes.

Much the same sort of comment comes from teachers who experience a curriculum project in action. Gleeson (1976) makes the point that,

> There is a tendency for curriculum developers to assume that the educational system acts in a systematized fashion, in that once ideas have been fed into it from the top (inputs of structured materials, resources, methods) these may then be processed through various channels to the grass roots at the bottom (output: classrooms). Such hierarchical assumptions of 'development' assume a split between experts and classroom teachers.

Under such conditions teachers experience a *Catch 22* situation with regard to the way their critical comments are processed by such experts – any criticism, according to the curriculum developer, was the result of 'not operating the thing properly'.

Consequently, unless knowledge is derived from the certified stock of the curriculum leader it is inadmissible in the area of design. And since design is an activity which is basically predictive, the argument is not about an actual outcome, but instead about a possible predicted outcome – the legitimation of design therefore depends upon a claim to possession of 'superior' knowledge and this, so the reasoning goes, is likely to be a more accurate predictor. Craft, intuitive or 'job' knowledge is deemed subjective and unreliable and responsible for all that might be currently astray with this area of curriculum design.

As we have already mentioned in the preceding chapter on educational design, this value works at denying the label of 'educational design' to those skills, crafts and knowledge which are not integrated into the existing power structures within education. Consequently, we find the issue of certification in curriculum central to establishing a secure niche within the power structures of education. According to the recommendations of the Association for Supervision and Curriculum Development a curriculum leader (in each school system) would have:

1. EXPERIENCE
   a. Minimum of two years' classroom teaching experience.
   b. Minimum of one-year leadership experience (such as department chairperson, elementary or secondary principal, internship, supervisor.
2. PREPARATION
   a. Certification as a teacher.
   b. Preparation in a related area (for example, additional preparation in elementary education).
   c. Completion or equivalent of an educational specialist degree leading to certification as a curriculum and instruction leader with courses and experience in the following areas:
      1) Curriculum, including the:
         (a) Theories of curriculum; models of curriculum development.
         (b) Knowledge and ability to apply skills of social research, including problem identification and the collection and analysis of data, in program planning.
         (c) Abilities to develop direction for a school system relating to local, state and national needs.
         (d) Possession of skills and abilities to construct educational programmes.
         (e) Abilities to identify appropriate criteria to evaluate programs.
      2) Instruction, including the:
         (a) Abilities to apply the theories of instruction and supervision to the improvement of instruction.
         (b) Knowledge of evaluative procedures to assume successful implementation of appropriate instructional procedures.
         (c) Recognition of differences in style and learning rates of students with varying backgrounds and cultural, ethnic, social, economic and religious backgrounds.
      3) Leadership, including:
         (a) Processes and purposes of organisation (organisational theory).

(b) Management skills to provide the human and material resources for facilitating curricular and instructional changes.

(c) Abilities to prioritize, in relation to district/state/ national goals, and possess decision making skills within a framework of sound human expertise and fiscal resources.

(d) Leadership skills of mobilizing the talents and abilities of co-workers (human relations skills included here).

(Speiker, 1976)

The reason for quoting this rather long section is to show the concern for certification and the global extent of the concerns of the curriculum leader. One is reminded of the earlier quoted 'model' of instructional technology which was concerned with the development (research, design, production, evaluation, support-supply, utilisation) of instructional components (messages, men, materials, devices, techniques, settings), and the management of that development (organisation, personnel) is a systematic manner with the goal of solving instructional problems! Notice also, the linking of management (euphemistically termed 'leadership') with theoretic-scientific knowledge.

As we noted earlier, the two key values of the designer's ideology are interrelated and interactive. This situation is especially the case within the area of curriculum. The second value, that of separating design from execution within a redefined totality, is a clear feature of the curriculum designer's position. Whatever else can be said about the nature of 'curriculum', one thing remains constant: curriculum thinking is directed towards 'wholes' or the 'total process'. Like educational technology, the term can be construed as broad as education itself. Curriculum is an organic whole with structures, roles and relationships; when characterised as a system, curriculum is a net of interrelated decisions which serve to define the 'ecology' for the educational 'organic whole'. And just as with the study of biological systems, it is scientific means which enable prediction and control of the system.

The means of redefining the whole is contained within the 'new language' of the curriculum designer. Teachers employ categories which relate to 'preparation' – this is not surprising as their concern is for teaching and learning, and, as teachers continually point out, such processes feed upon flexibility. Consequently, teachers are far more concerned for immediate aspects of classroom preparation – they are well aware of the fact that long-range plans are often made meaningless by the day-to-day discoveries made through implementing teaching and learning. Curriculum designers, on the other hand, reconceptualise the totality from the planning position – the source of authority now derives from educational management rather than teaching. Instead of describing the facets of classroom life in terms of teacher categories, the curriculum leader uses specialist jargon – terms such as 'situational analysis', 'goal formation', 'programme building', 'interpretation and implementation and monitoring', 'feedback', 'assessment and reconstruction' serve to describe and conceptualise. That this reconceptualisation clashes with teacher thinking and behaviour is beyond question. Clark and Yinger (1977), in an overview on research on teacher thinking, comment that,

> On the topic of teacher planning, the available literature suggests that teachers do not seem to follow the 'rational model' that is often prescribed in teacher training and in curriculum planning. In particular, teachers studied did not begin or guide their planning in relation to clearly specified objectives or goals. Rather, teacher planning seems to begin with the content to be taught and considerations about the setting in which teaching will take place. The focus then shifts to student involvement as a process objective.

Of course, the very fact that curriculum designers are involved in research on teacher thinking is of interest – the supposed intent is understanding why teachers behave as they do. However, researchers lament the fact that control through this research avenue may be tenuous at best due to the relatively loose connection between reported 'teacher thinking' and teacher behaviour!

Another approach to establishing the significance of the core values to the area of curriculum design is to consider the 'traditions' of the field. Again we shall employ the approach of considering data in terms of the 'world view' of the curriculum leader – that is, we are interested in an internalist explanation of historical development for the field. Internalist explanations are those constructed from a viewpoint which explains changes exclusively in terms of forces which are produced within and act only upon members of specialist groups. For the case of curriculum history an internalist view traces the changing ideas of the curriculum field through the professional associations, key curriculum figures, key texts and journals. Such changes are explained as if schools and educational policies were not influenced by 'external factors' such as social, economic and political movements.

Such 'internalist' analyses identify two phases in curriculum history – 'behaviouristic' (scientific curriculum-making) and 'technological procedures' (systems management). What is significant in terms of the developments within the field of curriculum is that, according to Franklin (1977) there exists a 'continuity between the early scientific curriculum-making movement and the systems-management procedures that dominate the contemporary field.' This continuity can well be considered as resulting from the stability of the core values already discussed; in fact, the two phases represent ways in which curriculum leaders (in their occupational role) adapt the core values to the climate of ideas available at the time. In this way Franklin (1977) comments (of the American situation),

> Curriculum workers do not typically question or challenge the approaches to curriculum issues dictated by the intellectual traditions of their field. Evidence of this exists in the basic similarities between the early scientific curriculum workers drawing on the scientific management movement, the principal industrial reform of their day, and in curriculum workers now turning for their ideas to the systems engineering procedures of the defense industry.

What is especially interesting is that the core values carry the conditions of the occupational role – a management role directed towards control. And, as middle managers, curriculum designers largely serve conservative political and social interests.

Quoting Franklin again,

> they [curriculum workers] are not aware of the belief shared by the majority of the formative theorists of the field: that the social function of the curriculum was to preserve what was thought to be a homogeneous American culture rooted in the values, attitudes and beliefs of a native middle class . . . they turned to the technological models already described because they saw in them mechanisms of social control that would enable the curriculum to function as an instrument of cultural uniformity.

Whether we can accept this analysis or not does not alter the point that the core values are directed towards control (of content and teachers within schooling and social and political control in the wider sense).

Another instance of the importance of the core values is given by Franklin's interpretation of the development of the occupational role of curriculum designers. In his opinion 'curriculum emerged as an occupation and a profession in the university when professors who originally held positions in departments of educational administration took on separate identities in departments of curriculum.' The need for role training in management (at all levels in the area of curriculum development) was obvious – national funding of innovations created a line-management situation and managers were required. This funding (in the American case) was large – as Maxson and Kraus (1979) report:

> From this initial grant, the NSF (National Science Foundation) expanded into the curriculum field rapidly, funding programs such as the Chemical Bond Approach (CBA) in 1957; the Biological Sciences Curriculum Study (BSCS) and Elementary School Science Project, both in 1959; and the University of Illinois Elementary School Science project in 1969.
>
> The total NSF budget in 1952 was $1,540,171; in 1959 this amount had increased by over $62 million to a total appropriation of $64,335,784. The expanded budget allowed a drastic increase in curriculum development to occur. In 1975 the foundation listed fifty-four curriculum projects receiving funding. According to NSF, funding for these programs totalled another $79,788,000. This means that over $186 million was spent by NSF in developing and implementing pre-college curricula, in the twenty years since 1956.

Consequently, new educational managers had to be found quickly, and training for future control over educational development became a new area in teacher training institutions and universities.

In general terms, teacher training institutions were less adaptive towards this trend as courses in 'methods' were very much linked to the classroom practices of teachers. Indeed, it is of considerable interest to trace the changing conception of 'methods' in such institutions. In some cases 'methods' became a wider concern to incorporate curriculum thinking but very much at a subject-based curriculum-development level; in other institutions courses in curriculum exist side by side with 'methods' courses often with considerable overlap of content. Further, where specific curriculum courses exist it is significant that many ignore the area of social, economic and political determinants of curriculum in preference for descriptive amounts of 'patterns of curriculum change' or 'curriculum in action' units or the like. The contradiction is evident – such courses aim at training curriculum managers (leaders), yet prefer to ignore the very ideological basis of management. The effect of a philosophy of liberal non-intervention is all too apparent!

Thus the approach of the curriculum designer is inherently political – the 'rationality' of his management models represent an attempt to by-pass the actual processes of curriculum change experienced at the worker (teacher) level. In actuality curriculum change at the 'chalk-face' is consequent upon some form of personal incorporation, challenge, rejection, re-ordering, readjusting . . . of values held by teachers. The curriculum manager attempts to by-pass such debate and challenge by authoritarian appeals to ideologically constrained justifications of curriculum 'decision-making'. The curriculum designer, in effect, makes an attempt to define educational design in apolitical terms, whereas every teacher knows from experience that the change of values inherent in proposed curriculum change is a political matter.

The next chapters look at measures which counter educational design, and are concerned with revaluing educational design from the viewpoint of the classroom floor.

References

BARTOO, E., SPEIKER, C. and STURGESS, A. 'Summary and Recommenda-
    tions', in Speiker, C. (ed), *Curriculum Leaders: Improving Their Influence*,
    (Association for Supervision and Curriculum Development, Washington,
    1976), p. 71
BEAUCHAMP, G. A. *Curriculum Theory*, (Kagg, Illinois, 1975), p. 150
Centre for Educational Research and Innovation. *Handbook on Curriculum
    Development*, (Organisation for Economic Cooperation and Development,
    Paris, 1975), p. 165
CLARK, C. M. and YINGER, R. J. 'Research on Teacher Thinking', *Curriculum
    Inquiry*, vol. 7, no. 4 (1977), pp. 279-305
Curriculum Development Centre. *Report on National Workshop*, (Australian
    Government Publishing Service, Canberra, April 1974)
ENGLISH, F. W. and KAUFMAN, R. A. *Needs Assessment: A Focus for Curri-
    culum Development*, (Association for Supervision and Curriculum Develop-
    ment, Washington DC, 1975), p. 1
FRANKLIN, B. M. 'Curriculum History: its Nature and Boundaries'. *Curriculum
    Inquiry*, vol. 7, no. 1 (1977), pp. 67-79
GLEESON, D. 'Experiencing a Curriculum Project', in Whitty, G. and Young,
    M. (eds), *Explorations in the Politics of School Knowledge*, (Nafferton,
    Driffield, UK, 1976)
HARLEN, W. 'A Stronger Teacher Role in Curriculum Development?' *Journal
    of Curriculum Studies*, vol. 9, no. 1 (1977), pp. 21-9
INGLIS, F. 'Ideology and the Curriculum: the Value Assumptions of System
    Builders', *Journal of Curriculum Studies*, vol. 6, no. 1 (1974), pp. 3-14
JAMES, D. 'Some Historical and Empirical Insights into the Relationship between

Curriculum Development and Educational Technology', *Probe A Journal of Educational Issues*, vol. 7, no. 2 (1978), pp. 4-15

KLIEBARD, H. M. 'The Rise of Scientific Curriculum Making and Its Aftermath', *Curriculum Theory Network*, vol. 5, no. 1 (1975), pp. 27-38

MARKLUND, S. 'Strategies of Educational Innovation', in McNally, P. J. (ed), *Queensland Conference on Curriculum Development*, (Ferguson, Brisbane, 1974), p. 13

MAXSON, M. M. and KRAUS, L. L. 'Curriculum Censorship in the Public School', *The Educational Forum*, vol. XLIII, no. 4 (1979), pp. 393-407

Northern Rivers College of Advanced Education. 'Graduate Diploma in Educational Studies: Curriculum Design and Development, Stage 3 Submission' (March 1979), p. 9, (unpublished document)

PINAR, W. F. 'The Reconceptualization of Curriculum Studies', *Curriculum Studies*, vol. 10, no. 3 (1978), pp. 205-14

SPEIKER, C. (ed), *Curriculum Leaders: Improving Their Influence*. (Association for Supervision and Curriculum Development, Washington, 1976), p. 5

WILKES, J. 'Theory in Educational Technology and Curriculum', *Programmed Learning and Educational Technology*, vol. 15, no. 1 (1978), pp. 79-82

YOUNG, M. 'The Rhetoric of Curriculum Development', in Whitty, G. and Young, M. (eds), *Explorations in the Politics of School Knowledge*, (Nafferton, Driffield, UK, 1976), p. 193

6 COUNTERING EDUCATIONAL DESIGN: THEORETICAL ISSUES

In this chapter we first look at ways to counter the arguments put forth by professional educational designers. Chapter 7 looks at ways in which teachers can begin to practise classroom alternatives which work against the designer's ideology. A final chapter extends these ideas and works towards developing personal styles of practice-theory dialectic. The aim of these latter chapters is to provide theoretical and practical information which can be applied by teachers in design areas so that they can become independent of the professional middle-managers who control educational design.

The chapters on countering educational design are based upon the belief that for those involved in teaching and learning at the 'classroom floor level' (both teachers and students), the meanings and purposes of the activities and events which make up the teaching and learning situation cannot be separated from the creative aspects of design and production of curricula, materials and evaluative mechanisms. Design in these areas is an expression of the meanings and purposes of the teaching and learning situation, and without this crucial element the teacher becomes a 'presenter' or 'implementer' acting out the purposes and meanings embodied in someone else's design.

Establishing a Practice-Theory Dialectic

Our approach in countering educational design could be termed 'developmental' - that is, stages of 'theory' and 'practice' progress according to the needs generated from the classroom floor. The source of such needs is the concern for providing 'good' teaching and learning situations. Within the classroom the teacher employs curricula, methods, materials, and evaluates teaching and learning - and, in adjusting such concerns to the needs, abilities and interests of students, teachers are creatively involved with educational design. Sometimes this means adapting, adopting or amending a resource or fitting together separate resources; at other times this means designing new curricula or producing materials or evaluating in new ways. But whatever the design activity, we work from the basis that a need arises from the context of classroom teaching and learning.

At a theoretical level the development of a personal practice-theory dialectic begins with knowing about ideas which serve to counter the two ideological core values of the professional educational designers. Such ideas are 'tools' which can be used to counter the specific arguments put forth by educational designers in justifying their control over the area of design. The counter-arguments, taken issue by issue, are given in order that teachers can match the ideological claims put forth by professional designers. Arguing against the core values of the designers is a 'first step' to gaining the offensive in the area of educational design. We have already touched upon some aspects of such arguments in the chapter on educational design, and it is now time to extend this initial contact.

Design and Rational Action

The first of the core values is concerned with an insistence upon knowledge derived from rational sources. Embedded in this value is a particular view of rational conduct – a view which assumes that rational action can be pre-planned before an event begins. This concept of rational action rejects the notion that rationality might reside in the choices that are made as the action unfolds.

The counter-view of rational action that is employed here is not at all new – it draws from the writings of Michael Oakeshott and Michael Polanyi. What is significant is that both these writers are either ignored (as in the case of educational technology) or often given scant attention (as with curriculum design). Perhaps one reason for this is that within the political arena of education these ideas can be used to assign authority to teachers.

According to Oakeshott's (1962) analysis of conventional rational action,

> The appearance which conduct would tend to assume if it conformed to this [conventional] notion of 'rationality' is not in any doubt. Activity would be bent towards the performance of actions in pursuit of preconceived and formulated ends, actions determined wholly by the ends sought and from which fortuitous and unwanted consequences had, so far as possible, been excluded. Its aim would be, first, to establish a proposition, to determine a purpose to be pursued, secondly, to determine the means to be employed to achieve that (and no other) end, and, thirdly to act. Human

behaviour would appear to be broken up into a series of individual actions performed in pursuit of these ends. The unprejudiced consideration of every project would take place of policy, precedent and prescription would be avoided (so far as possible) in determining enterprise, and the man who had a formula would come to oust the man who had none.

Rational conduct, in conventional terms, is dependent upon what is done before an action is undertaken. An activity is rational when it is generated in a certain manner. This approved mode of conduct involves imagining and choosing a purpose, then clarifying and defining the purpose and selecting ways of achieving the purpose; such processes are assisted by 'emptying the mind' to remove preconceptions so that this mode of conduct can become independent of the restraints of tradition and other 'external factors'. Indeed, such processes are independent of the activity itself as they are preliminaries to action! So powerful is this idea of conduct that its directions for action are universal in that when others apply such procedures they will be led to the same conclusions and actions.

Now Oakeshott objects to this account of rational conduct because it is not a satisfactory account of any sort of conduct. Further, there is the practical danger that this account will indeed confuse activity by leading people to conceptualise activity in terms of this misleading account.

By now it should be quite clear that the conventional philosophical notion of rational conduct is at the basis of many of the models and systematic approaches used in curriculum design and educational technology. It is this account of rational action which, as Shaw (1976) notes in the area of curriculum, has 'compelling qualities of clarity, simplicity, and articulation'. It is an 'expository device' and not the description of a real activity. Also, it is this formalised account which looks very much like the so called 'scientific method' - and, as Kuhn (1962) comments of such accounts of scientific activity contained in text books,

> Inevitably, however, the aim of such books is persuasive and pedagogic; a concept of science drawn from them is no more likely to fit the enterprise that produced them than an image of a national culture drawn from a tourist brochure or a language text.

Likewise, accounts of 'rational' educational design contained in courses and texts in educational technology and curriculum simply do not reflect the realities of educational design in each of these areas. Put another way, a reconstituted or *post hoc* logic for design does not measure the 'logic in use' of the activity of design.

To understand why this concept of 'rational' action is misleading and false involves considerable philosophical analysis. The argument leads to considering 'conceptions of mind' and 'ways of knowing'. We shall try to by-pass much of the detail and concentrate on those parts of the argument which relate directly to our attack upon the core values of the educational designers. For those interested in following up such arguments in detail, Oakeshott (1962) and Polanyi (1958 and 1969) may be consulted.

'Doing' Educational Design

The basis of our argument against the core values of educational designers is expressed by Oakeshott (1962).

> *Doing* anything both depends upon and exhibits knowing how to do it; and though part (but never the whole) of knowing how to do it can subsequently be reduced to knowledge in the form of propositions (and possibly to ends, rules and principles), these propositions are neither the spring of the activity nor are they in any direct sense regulative of the activity.

This notion of 'doing' insists that actions *cannot* be directed only by predetermined principles or rules - a thorough knowledge of rules is no guarantee that we can pursue the activity to which they refer. Indeed, there are times when we can successfully carry out an activity yet be unable to recount the 'rules' of the activity. Of course, there also exists the further possibility that the 'rules' cannot be explicitly stated!

Perhaps an example will make this clear. Let us take 'doing' educational design. To be specific, let us consider designing a curriculum unit.

Now any number of educational texts will provide principles of curriculum-unit design - there are techniques for stating aims and objectives, principles for the selection of content, principles for the selection of teaching strategies and techniques, principles for making decisions about sequencing learning, principles for the selection and development of materials, principles on which to evaluate, principles for this, principles for that - a 'never ending' list of such principles forms the basis of curriculum design. Yet, search as you may, there is little about knowing how and when to apply such principles! That is, it is impossible to actually do curriculum design armed only with these principles. Where are we to look for the missing ingredient which assists 'doing' curriculum design? Certainly not in the aims that have been predetermined, as they tell us nothing about how or when. The only possible area must be in the *activity itself*. Consequently, it is impossible to completely pre-plan an activity - we cannot know how or when to apply such knowledge until the activity is in progress. But, more importantly, this means that 'rational conduct' cannot depend completely upon a 'mode of conduct' exhibited before the event unfolds. 'Rational' must therefore refer, at least in part, to a quality of the activity itself. What then, is this quality?

Our answer can only be that the activity in question is judged 'appropriate' in terms of the context in which it is carried out - in Oakeshott's terms, it shows a 'faithfulness to the knowledge we have of how to conduct the specific activity we are engaged in.'

Now this conception of rational action sides completely with the practitioner - only the practitioner can judge the course of action (appropriate to the 'traditions' of this activity) as an activity proceeds. Those involved in 'rational design', those who remove themselves from 'doing' an activity, lose the right to make judgements since they are not involved with the activity. Their involvement is with 'planning' only - consequently, the planner's source of authority over practice cannot come from practice. Thus, those 'professionals' involved with educational design derive their authority over teachers from sources outside of teaching and learning.

This notion of rational conduct places intuition, craft knowledge and traditions of the activity central to 'doing' the activity. Consequently, doing curriculum-unit design becomes immersed both within the context in which design is practised and the identifiable traditions which contain evaluative standards. Further, it is only through carrying out curriculum-unit design in a particular context that we can enter into the traditions of the activity. Under such conditions theoretic knowledge cannot be used as the means of legitimating control over the processes of unit design.

Tradition and Rational Action

The mention of 'tradition' brings a new element into our argument. The use of this concept is enough to sorely provoke rationalists who believe tradition to be something which man uses to replace reason. Such rationalists characterise tradition as something which impedes 'rational conduct' – traditional forces are linked with superstition or an attachment to an outmoded past for the sake of the past. Tradition represents forces opposed to change and progress.

Now it is not this conception of tradition that we wish to use here. Instead, we follow Szacki's (1969) work and characterise tradition as a 'dynamic' element which interacts with values. In essence, this concept of tradition is based around the following statements:

1. tradition frequently happened to be an object of complex intellectual operations;
2. it is said that we have to do with tradition when a part of the heritage is subject to valuation by the group from a special point of view;
3. when studying tradition we are interested not in what has been preserved from the past, but in elements of social heritage that are still being subject to valuations by the group;
4. 'rationalization' of tradition . . . eliminates it *qua* tradition.

Now what is important here is that this notion of tradition is linked with how groups value things from special viewpoints. And one thing that is quite clear from current anthropological studies of 'teacher culture' is that traditions belonging to teachers as a group do exist and are quite 'solid'. Such traditions enable teachers to evaluate and work with the complex intellectual operations behind 'doing' such things as curriculum design, materials design and the like. Indeed, the 'idiom of an activity' such as design is embodied in such traditions.

Consequently, 'rational conduct' in the area of educational design cannot rest upon a theoretic knowledge which, to give the impression of certainty and universality, is put in acontextual, apolitical and asocial terms. Instead, teachers can point out that the essence of educational design is contained within *their* traditions of practice in this area. Change is something which requires a creative revaluation of 'traditions of activity' – a revaluation which concerns teachers as individuals and groups.

Such conceptions which place central importance upon craft or traditional knowledge counter the extreme 'rationalism' embodied in approaches which are based upon the two core values already outlined. The ideas above will be used in examples of counter arguments relating to specific areas (e.g. systems approach). Also, we will need to apply these ideas in outlining the significance of the second of the core values concerning the separation of design from execution. This dichotomy between doing and thinking will be denied, partly through an extension of the above analysis.

The second core value of the educational designer, that of insisting upon dividing the teaching and learning totality into a design phase and an execution phase, is first considered from a political (rather than philosophical) viewpoint. This division of 'educational labour' is first and foremost a means of preventing teacher access to the teaching and learning totality. The definition of the design task and the implementation task contain within them the intended managerial relation. The authority embodied in this relation stems from control over a redefined totality from the viewpoint of design.

As this is a political viewpoint, countering this value depends upon action of a political kind. Where changes are enforced through bureaucratic means, various teacher strategies for coping with change have been observed; Wolcott (1977) provides examples of both compliance and resistance exhibited by teachers in dealing with unwanted change. Other avenues involve practices which deny this separation of design from execution – they involve self-sufficiency in design, production and evaluation in the school setting. As such avenues result from developing alternative strategies in educational design, we will return to them in the final chapter. For now, let us return to a theoretical-philosophical stance which supplies the basis of argument against this value.

Doing and Thinking

The dichotomy between doing and thinking has its grounds in a dichotomy in forms of knowledge and ways of knowing. All teachers know of this dichotomy. It also provides fundamental difficulties for courses in teacher training. There are few teachers who have not questioned the theory-practice split. The theoretic knowledge supplied through 'educational studies' and the craft knowledge supplied by the teacher as a practitioner seem to be pitted against each other. All beginning teachers at some stage have been given the advice to forget what they have learned in training institutions and attend to becoming 'apprenticed' within the school! The perceived irrelevance of theory to practice is also a constant student criticism.

This dichotomy is a necessary part of educational design as practised by the professional designers. Managerial authority is derived from assuming a derivative relationship between theory and practice – it is theory which directs practice. The reason for this is that theoretical knowledge is assumed more reliable, objective and valuable – further, theoretical knowledge has less of the inertia of tradition in that it sits above, and consequently has the capacity to change faster than, practice. Changing practice is seen as being a more difficult task than changing theoretical perspectives.

According to the managerial ideology two sorts of 'knowledge' exist. The first type is susceptible to explicit and precise formulation (variously termed technical, objective or operational knowledge). The other and different type exists only in use and often cannot be put into rules or precepts (variously called practical, personal or intuitive knowledge). Where the power relation between manager and worker is supposedly 'objectified' through the possession of 'superior knowledge', it is clear that the first type of knowledge must be cast as superior to the second. This is a consequence of the fact that a manager manages, and need not actually carry out the activity he manages; his stock of practical knowledge relates to managing rather than the actual activity he manages.

For purposes of control, knowledge of the second type, which is clearly related to the traditions of an activity, is inadmissible. Management, in its 'scientific' guise, therefore attempts to generate a set of operative precepts – rules of the type that state: to cause x to happen, you must do y.

Now it is quite clear that prescriptions for action cannot rest upon such a basis. As we have already seen, it is only when other rules and precepts (of a normative or 'value' kind) are linked with such operative precepts and applied within the traditions of activity (employing 'practical' knowledge) that we can begin to understand 'rational conduct' within activity. The managerial position retains power over 'normative' or value concerns (in the act of managing), and does not consider the possession of practical knowledge as a legitimate claim for control over an activity. If such knowledge were admitted, control over what constitutes 'rational' or 'approved' action can only reside with those who actually carry out action.

Consequently, the managerial position requires a reconceptualisation of action or practice which can justify the omission of such knowledge. Completeness must therefore be seen in *theoretic* terms and these alone – the various models and systems approaches which abound in the area of educational design are the results of such an ideological position.

All of this points to the way that the two core values of the educational designer interact to form a self-justifying ideological position. Under such conditions rejecting either value is to counter both – also, rejection upon philosophical grounds has obvious political consequences. Likewise, actions based upon alternative positions which deny these core values will be largely rejected by institutionalised education and the school, as both give tacit approval to such values.

However, for now, let us look at how our counter-arguments can be applied to specific instances within educational design. We take a simple 'systems' approach to unit design first.

Systems Approach to 'Unit' Design

Educational technologists use this approach to justify educational design. The first step is to carry out an analytic breakdown of the content into units of such a size that behavioural objectives can be written. Thus, learning is divided into categories, and within each category evidence of learning can be seen through the learner being able to carry out a specific behaviour. Within each category behaviours are listed in a hierarchical fashion, with more complex learning being evident when a learner displays a behaviour appropriate to the higher hierarchical division. It is assumed that, in order to achieve behaviours linked with complex learning tasks, the learner must be able to show the behaviours appropriate to all lower-task levels.

This rationale sets specific objectives related to broader aims – it also specifies the more complex aim in terms of a number of objectives which comprise the aim. Further, the educational technologist claims that the act of specification provides the key to the selection of means – that is, once the objectives are clearly defined the way to achieve them (in terms of sequencing, production of materials, selection of media) becomes evident. According to Gerlach's and Ely's (1971) systematic approach to instruction there are ten elements that must operate within the system. These are –

1. specification of objectives and
2. selection of content,
3. the assessment of entering behaviours,
4. the strategy which will be employed,
5. the organisation of students into groups,
6. the allocation of time,
7. the allocation of learning spaces, and
8. the selection of appropriate learning resources.

Once the design of the previous elements has been established,

9. the evaluation of teacher and learner performance follows with
10. an analysis of feedback by the teacher and learner.

In diagrammatic form –

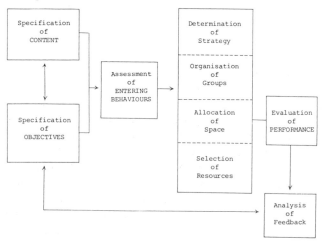

(From Gerlach and Ely, 1971, p. 29)

After a pre-test (entering behaviour) the various design decisions relating to media selection, production, resource use and evaluation are to be outlined in terms of theoretic knowledge derived from studies in human information-processing, perception, learning theory, art and advertising principles, media research and the like – in this way strategies are designed and materials are produced which should meet the learning specifications embodied in the objectives. The final stage of evaluation requires a congruence between observed student behaviours after the treatment and the behaviours embodied in the declared objectives. If the students meet these criteria established during the design phase, then the teaching and learning strategies and materials are deemed successful.

The argument of the educational technologist rests upon the use of theoretic knowledge in a thorough, systematic fashion – and as the objectives are 'testable', the system can be adjusted to achieve such objectives. The system provides a complete description and working model for the instructional process.

A critique of this argument can be readily supplied. First, using our previous analysis of 'rational conduct' we can reject this schema as it does not describe design activities in any real fashion. That is, we can insist that this skeleton which supposedly characterises an approach to instruction, is a stylised *post hoc* rationalisation of the activity of design.

This argument can be strengthened by considering more specific issues. Thus a teacher might well challenge the educational technologist on the following:

(1)   If success is merely the measure of whether the objectives (which may be seriously limited in their scope) are met, how do you know that the procedures and strategies have been 'correctly' chosen? If it is possible that another strategy or procedure can achieve the objectives, is it possible to choose between these two means? Further, if any 'intuitive' construction meets the criteria, can such approaches be any worse than the pre-planned effort? The answer to this latter question will display the ideological commitment of the educational technologist – and, further, the justification is likely to be philosophically naïve. At this point the various arguments concerning 'rational conduct' and the role of craft knowledge within a tradition of activity can be employed.

(2)   What happens if, after the instruction, the criteria are not met? Does this infer that the techniques were incorrectly applied or the analytic processes deficient? The answer given by the educational technologist is generally that the procedures are not at fault. Nor are they incorrectly applied. This reply preserves that status of procedures, and means that the reason for students not achieving the objectives lies primarily with the students. (Here we assume that various attempts at adjusting the system have failed.) Consequently, adjustments must be made to the initial objectives for this human factor. But once this admission is made there is the way open to state that teachers using their approach to design can also ensure 'success' by adjusting the objectives to suit the outcomes.

(3) A more 'sophisticated' approach to instructional design considers the eventuality of a mismatch between the declared objectives and the observed performance. The argument is that the system can be retuned in the light of an analysis of the design – a recycling through this retuned system will now bring a congruence between pre-planned objectives and performance. Indeed, this approach has been given certified evaluation phases – a formative evaluation is associated with 'first trials' of the system and after amendment a summative evaluation occurs.

Again, this argument is easily criticised. It is well realised by educational technologists (but often left largely unstated) that systems analysis in its strict sense is inapplicable to educational problems. The reason for this is that systems analysis depends upon the existence of discrete identifiable sub-systems which have a limited number of interactions between themselves. Such sub-systems should be uniquely defined in terms of specific boundary conditions; further, the mode of interaction between sub-systems should be such that the interaction itself can be predicted and controlled. Without these conditions the whole notion of controlled change or 'tuning' a system breaks down. Also, without definite sub-systems no internal structure exists, and the object under description is more akin to a single mass of interconnected and mutually interactive parts.

Clearly, much of what goes on in schooling and instruction is too intertwined to allow the existence of discrete sub-systems, while most of the interactions lack quantifiable variables. So, at best, adjustments of such systems are 'intuitive'. In much the same way teachers make 'intuitive' adjustments to their design problems. Further, the more the educational technologist argues for feedback loops, the more interactive and 'circular' his system becomes, and the more difficult to be predictive about the effects of any changes brought about to a section of the system.

Basically, each criticism leads to the role of 'craft knowledge', tradition and the 'idiom of an activity' in applying such theoretic structures to classroom practice. The inadequacies of theoretic structures are easily revealed, and a realisation of this provides an effective counter to those who would wish to manage the efforts of the classroom teacher. Under the guise of technique there is an ideological conception of the teaching/learning process – criticism of both the technique and the ideological values proves an effective counter measure.

Media Selection in Educational Design

Let us take another example – that of media selection. This is a crucial area of educational design; the professional educational technologist, for example, trades upon his ability to select the 'optimum' medium for a given learning or instructional task. This selection task is important for two reasons. First, as middle management the educational technologist is expected to assist management with 'executive decisions' about accountability; and secondly, the educational technologist claims theoretic knowledge which gives control in this area. On the first matter the management ideology of educational technology comfortably accommodates the concerns of accountability. Media selection based upon a host of factors such as knowledge of hardware and software, production costs, reliability, depreciation and learning effectiveness is used to forecast whether a particular medium will work with regard to certain explicit criteria (objectives, physical conditions, cost analysis, etc.). Such information is a necessary part of bureaucratic 'rational planning'.

Indeed, some ten years ago when educational technology was more heavily media-oriented, this problem of media selection was viewed as central to establishing the relevance of this developing area. In practical terms this problem is quite central, as where an educational technologist is unable to specify the correct 'tool' (medium) for a job (educational design) he is hardly in a position to claim management know-how. It was soon realised that selection of a medium based on a simple cost factor was a procedure which required no real specialist or management knowledge. Consequently, to be able to justify selection for educational design upon grounds other than economic became a key issue with obvious role implications.

The numerous and diverse approaches to the problem of media selection illustrate its significance. Early attempts (mainly in the late sixties and early seventies) gathered together what was known about media properties and attempted to construct selection matrices. The idea was to make a matrix which classified media according to a number of properties. These properties were described in a wide variety of ways. Boucher *et al.* (1973) used presentation, student response and instructional-strategy parameters; Briggs (1970) employed learner characteristics, task requirements, materials and transmission; Gagne (1965) attempted to use his instructional functions of presenting the stimulus, directing attention, providing a model of expected performance, furnishing external prompts, guiding thinking, inducing transfer, assessing attainments and providing feedback; Levie (1975) describes media attributes in terms of sign-vehicle characteristics, realism-cue characteristics, sensory-channel characteristics, locus-of-control characteristics and response-acceptance characteristics; Tosti and Ball (1969) employ the idea of a 'presentation form' which has the six dimensions of stimulus encoding form, stimulus duration, response-demand form, response-demand frequency, management form and management frequency.

These are but some of the more significant theoretical attacks upon the problem of media selection. This brief outline has been given to indicate the ingenuity and intensity of this work. Hawkridge (1973) points out that in the United States alone, over two thousand studies 'researched' this area. This onslaught yielded little, and today the educational technologist has almost given up the search for explicit media-selection schemes. This highly significant area proves a considerable source of embarrassment. Heidt (1975), for example, points out that 'most classifications claim initially to be applicable to practical instruction, but such claims prove to be illusory as soon as a teacher or other practitioner tries to use them for a specific problem.'

Despite this setback, texts in educational technology still prescribe media-selection schemes. Most texts argue that the selection of a medium for a particular instructional task is a function of two prime considerations: the behavioural objectives and the properties of the medium. The different media have different properties in relation to how they present information (provide the stimulus), how students can interact with them (responses), and how a teacher can use them to manage a presentation. The first task is therefore to reduce the content to behavioural objectives in a search for student behaviours and inferred teacher behaviours. Also what is to be presented (the stimulus) appears within the content part of a behavioural objectives statement. Once decisions have been made on what sorts and types of stimuli, what sorts, types and how many responses, and what management conditions, the next step is to match these conditions with one or more media.

At other times a more pragmatic approach is taken where a mix of 'research findings', cost analysis, 'learning factors' and production variables is considered in a selection. Now such arguments are often presented as 'technical matters' – that is, media selection is cast as an applied science. Once the learning specifications are refined the matter of media selection is supposedly solved!

An effective counter to this is to point out the deficiencies of rule-based approaches to action. Such approaches employ maxims which often represent 'correlations' between variables (often derived from highly suspect 'research') or pragmatic observations. Rules of this kind can be presented in table form or as statements. For example, suppose medium X had the following properties:

Medium	Advantages	Disadvantage
X	A	B

The media-selection rule then becomes: where there is an absence of B medium X can be used to an A advantage.

In a like fashion, educational technologists have generated rules to cover media and 'advantages' such as the learning of principles, guiding thinking, motivating, flexibility of use, furnishing external prompts . . . and a host of other variables. But, as we have already seen, a knowledge of such rules often means little – even if such maxims were theoretically sound, their application requires a knowledge of context on which they are to be applied and a 'craft knowledge' concerning when and how to apply such rules. As well as this criticism, Heidt (1976) contends that, 'The connections of media with other factors of the teaching and learning process however, are too complex to be covered appropriately by a single taxonomy or simple rating system'. Indeed, such rule-styled information quoted by educational technologists is likely either to be highly suspect (as for instructional functions and media) or merely platitudinous and obvious (as for audience size and media). Clearly, the inadequacy of such explicit procedures is all too obvious. In designing materials teachers necessarily have a more intimate understanding of the particular contextual situation in which the audio-visual aid is to be used. Teachers can therefore rightly claim that their media-selection decisions (provided there are no obvious 'technical' errors) are equally as sound as those of the educational technologist. Where the educational technologist begins to claim superior 'intuitive' skills it is easy to point out that teachers actually apply craft-knowledge from the solid foundation of practice – often, the educational technologist is in essence attempting to manage what he has not 'experienced' himself!

Behavioural Objectives

Another design issue which appears within both educational technology and curriculum is that of behaviourism. To the educational technologist, for example, the stating of behavioural objectives provides the key to effective media selection, content sequencing and evaluation. In the area of curriculum design behaviourism provides one method of specifying objectives.

Standard texts in educational technology present behaviourism (the psychological study of behaviours) as 'scientific truth'. True, there may be some resistance by teachers to accept the application of such truths, but this is explained by their inadequate ideas about curriculum or instruction! Now what is particularly interesting about this is that despite the philosophical, psychological and political attacks upon the assumptions of behaviourism, this approach is still recommended and prescribed as 'knowledge that teachers should use'.

One reason why behaviourism is supposed to be so useful for teachers is that behavioural objectives can be ranked in 'levels of difficulty' – and, when teaching a topic, it is essential that pre-requisite behaviours are achieved first. In this way instruction is designed as a sequence of levels of behaviour – knowledge of specifics is to precede comprehension which is necessary for application and so on. The most well-known (and perhaps the only) taxonomy of objectives that teacher training institutions give to their students is that by Bloom. The exercise of stating objectives and sequencing them becomes a technique to be learnt within educational technology or curriculum courses.

This is not the place to detail the arguments against behaviourism – for teachers who are interested in following this further, one of the best reviews is by Macdonald-Ross (1975). However, by way of a quick counter, the following information could be useful. First, point out the values behind such approaches. As Ormell (1974) notes,

> the [Bloom] taxonomy reflects an attitude to education which may be described as 'materialist'. It speaks over and over again of education as the handling of communications. The picture which seems to be permanently present in the background is of the student as handling *material*: acquiring it in bits (knowledge of specifics), turning it over (comprehension), allocating it (application), dissecting it (analysis), putting it together in new ways (synthesis) and comparing the results with other results or established criteria (evaluation).

So, the first point here is that it is possible to argue against the materialist position and the view of communication which it uses. Briefly, communication according to the materialist scheme is more a matter of cause and effect (stimulus and response) than meaning and intention. This conception of communication has serious deficiencies. In the final chapter this cause and effect (process) versus meaning and intentionality (praxis) split is discussed.

A second point to bring up is the supposed technical nature of taxonomies. In themselves they reflect values – for example, it is well known that the levels of activity in the Bloom taxonomy reflect the 'social ladder' of a production-oriented society. As Ormell notes, there is a correspondence between the 'type of person' and main skill employed in the 'type of job'. Politicians, at the top of the ladder, employ evaluation, civil servants and directors use synthesis, scientists and technologists analyse; managers are linked with application, the skilled man with comprehension and the unskilled man with a knowledge of specifics.

This point can be used to attack the value-neutral, 'scientific' approach of educational design. If sequencing is based upon the sorts of 'sequences' which fit a meritocratic view of society it is certainly not a neutral tool! Consequently, authority over the design process is not a measure of a superior theoretic position – instead of depending upon 'factual' knowledge it rests upon social values.

A third and important point is to ask where behavioural objectives come from. At the level of job-skill training answers are readily forthcoming – look at the skills required for a specific job, validate this list and arrange them in levels. Does the same apply for education and schooling? To answer this question educational technologists (or curriculum leaders) are faced with two significant choices: they claim either that training models are all that is necessary for teaching and learning or that there are some aspects of education and schooling which defy a behavioural interpretation. Soon the discussion comes to centre around the relevance of objectives (Macdonald-Ross, 1972) – here teachers can claim that through their necessarily more extensive contact with their students they are able to design teaching and learning situations which serve relevant objectives.

These examples by no means exhaust the counter arguments to behaviouristic approaches to design. Once discussion begins other points arise – behavioural objectives support a totally inadequate model of teacher-student interactions, they foster trivialisation of objectives, they focus attention on end points rather than journeys, they have a converging influence upon thinking, and so on.

In Chapter 7 we move to the area of practical issues, and examine further ways of countering educational design.

References

BOUCHER, B. G., GOTLIEB, M. J. and MORGAN CANDER, M. L. *Handbook and Catalogue for Instructional Media Selection*, (Educational Technology Publications, New Jersey, 1973)

BRIGGS, L. J. *Handbook of Procedures for the Design of Instruction*, (American Institute for Research, Pittsburg, 1970)

GAGNE, R. M. *The Conditions of Learning*, (Holt, Rinehart & Winston, New York, 1965)

GERLACH, V. S. and ELY, D. P. *Teaching and Media: A Systematic Approach*, (Prentice-Hall, New Jersey, 1971)

HAWKRIDGE, D. G. 'Media Taxonomies and Media Selection' in Budgett, R. and Leedham, J. (eds), *Aspects of Educational Technology VII*, (Pitman, Bath, 1973)

HEIDT, E. 'In Search of a Media Taxonomy: Problems of Theory and Practice', *British Journal of Educational Technology*, vol. 1, no. 6, (1975), pp. 4-22

HEIDT, E. *Instructional Media and the Individual Learner*, (Kogan Page, London, 1976 (translation 1978)

KUHN, T. S. *The Structure of Scientific Revolutions*. Second Edition. (University of Chicago Press, Chicago, 1962)

LEVIE, W. H. 'How to Understand Instructional Media', *Viewpoints*, vol. 51, no. 5, (1975), pp. 25-42

MACDONALD-ROSS, M. 'Behavioural Objectives: A Critical Review' in Golby, M. *et al. Curriculum Design*, (Croom Helm, London, 1975), pp. 355-86

MACDONALD-ROSS, M. 'Behavioural Objectives and the Structure of Knowledge' in Austwick, K. and Harris, N. D. C. (eds), *Aspects of Educational Technology VI*, (Pitman, London, 1972), pp. 38-47

OAKESHOTT, M. *Rationalism in Politics*, (Methuen, London, 1962)

ORMELL, C. P. 'Bloom's Taxonomy and the Objectives of Education', *Educational Research*, vol. 17, no. 1, (1974), pp. 3-17

POLANYI, M. *Personal Knowledge*, (Routledge and Kegan Paul, London, 1958)

POLANYI, M. 'Knowing and Being' in Greene, M. (ed), *Knowing and Being: Essays by Michael Polanyi*, (Routledge and Kegan Paul, London, 1969)

SHAW, K. E. 'Paradigms or Contested Concepts', *British Journal of Educational Technology*, vol. 7, no. 2, (1976), pp. 18-24

SZACKI, J. 'Three Concepts of Tradition', *The Polish Sociological Bulletin*, vol. 2, (1969), pp. 2-31

TOSTI, D. T. and BALL, J. R. 'A Behavioural Approach to Instructional Design and Media Selection', *A. V. Communication Review*, vol. 17, no. 1, (1969), pp. 5-25

WOLCOTT, H. F. *Teachers vs. Technocrats*. (Centre for Educational Policy and Management, University of Oregon, 1977), p. 198

7 COUNTERING EDUCATIONAL DESIGN: PRACTICAL ISSUES

This chapter looks at some practical issues which arise when teachers start down pathways towards self-sufficiency in educational design and production.

Chapter 6 can derive full meaning only through confronting its theoretical issues in the realm of the practical. That is, much of the previous chapter should be used and judged only in the light of whether the 'theorising' helps to make sense of the practical realities of the teaching and learning situation from the classroom floor.

It is clear that the practical issues of this chapter cannot be considered as being separate from the theoretical issues of the previous. Knowing about theoretical issues in educational design is, at most, but half-way towards countering educational design. When integrated with, and changed according to, the practice of design, it is indeed half-way; but without this interactive relationship such theoretical knowledge counts for very much less.

Thus, countering educational design is seen to rest upon a progressive interchange between 'doing' and 'theorising'. Each nurtures the other: sometimes doing will prompt the need for theorising, while at other times 'theorising' will suggest how to act. This dialectic relationship is established within the particular context of the classroom and experienced without a theory-practice split. The one and the same teacher is the conceiver and user of educational design.

Further, in developing this dialectic approach it must be remembered that we reject the idea that a single unique solution to problems in educational design exists. The rationalist-management approach of searching for the technical-based solution is inappropriate for the practical deliberations required of educational design. Instead, we look towards the development of practical reasoning by confronting problems in educational design within the context and traditions of the classroom.

The most direct approach to countering educational design through practical issues begins by considering audio-visual hardware. Hardware is the equipment required to produce or reproduce the content (contained in the software). Thus, a projector is an example of a piece of hardware, while the film used to capture images, which are displayed by using the projector, is the accompanying software.

Knowing the operational procedures and the capacities of such aids is an obvious starting point for self-sufficiency in design and production. Often it is through the use of 'play-back' hardware such as 16-mm and 35-mm projectors that teachers develop an interest in 'production' hardware such as movie and still cameras. For example, using an existing resource (say a photographic-slide set) may cause a teacher to analyse the content and the methodological aspects associated with this aid, and the various benefits and limitations of using this approach are assessed in terms of the contextual situation. This may result in a reordering of the content (which may lead to practical problems associated with curriculum), or a desire to supplement the materials to meet personal and contextual needs (which may lead to production of photographic materials), or a feeling of dissatisfaction with methodological procedures (which may cause a restructuring of priorities within the teaching and learning situation or perhaps change evaluative procedures).

So, the first and obvious thing to do is to use existing resources whether they be unstructured or in kit form. The second thing is to become familiar with all forms of play-back and production hardware.

Knowing about hardware is not difficult. Any number of manuals can supply the information necessary to use such equipment, but perhaps the best source is the instructions provided by the maker. As well as this it is a good idea to go to some encyclopedia of inventions (or similar) to obtain some working knowledge of the technological or scientific principles which underlie such operations.

A knowledge of the basic capacities and capabilities of hardware/software combinations needs to be based upon experience through use. For example, use of the process of recording might motivate a teacher to find out more about its educational uses in solving timetabling problems, or more importantly, control over content through editing. Another aspect associated with using hardware/software combinations is the degree to which they can be used as a teacher-centred or learner-centred tool. Often, the one and the same piece of equipment can be used either way – for example, an overhead projector may be a highly teacher-centred tool when used as an 'electric blackboard', yet becomes a learner-centred tool when used by students for information retrieval or as a means of displaying and reporting their work.

Experience through use is likewise fundamental to understanding media-selection problems. Theoretical tables will establish the fact that television (say) is a fixed-pace, fixed-sequence medium; recounting such means little until experiencing the desire to reorder content or to 'slow down' a programme to suit the requirements of particular students. Indeed, most media-selection choices revolve around obvious methodological capacities inherent in the medium – and it is only through producing and using media that skills in this area can be developed. A view from the classroom floor supports the idea that valid media justification is carried out by teachers when they weigh up the benefits and limitations for the particular context within which materials are to be produced and used.

Practical Issues – Initial Contact

To summarise: a 'first phase' in this developmental process might include:

(1)   familiarisation with hardware and perhaps some knowledge of the underlying technology. This familiarisation ranges from knowing how to replenish duplicator spirit to the use of single-reflex cameras on copy stands and TV porta-packs. In most instances the level of operational skill and information necessary for using such equipment is minimal, as manufacturers tend to work towards fool-proofing their equipment. This stage involves gaining access to the equipment and software, which, in itself, may prove quite difficult. As a practical point it is essential to establish, as far as is possible, 'open access' to the production resources available. One possible way to get a foot in the door is to demonstrate competence in using productional equipment.

(2)   the use of materials and equipment as aids to lessons in order to gain experience of the benefits and limitations of audio-visual approaches. This will perhaps lead to greater reliance upon resource-based teaching and learning, and eventually cause significant changes in perceived teacher roles.

(3)   the production of materials which support a lesson or a series of lessons. Such productions require no special considerations, and can be viewed as a natural extension of teacher production of print materials.

Production possibilities are seen to arise from the felt needs of the classroom, and in many instances the need to produce materials arises in the form of a 'solution' to an unanticipated learning problem. It is important not to overlook the catalytic effect of using media approaches – a particular visual or a special film or video-tape may produce unintended and divergent responses which demand attention. This, in turn, may suggest further production or resource-based learning as follow-up.

Further Practical Experience

This first phase has now provided initial experiences in the areas of production and use of teaching and learning materials. So far much of the production is piecemeal and in response to specific teaching or learning tasks. The next phase moves much closer to educational design as it is seen by the professional designer. In this phase we can no longer be solely concerned with the instruments of production and their capabilities – instead, we work towards applying the theoretical and practical skills in an extended sense. Further, with our rejection of the management ideology we rejoin 'conception' with 'execution' within educational practice – in this way, issues of materials production and curriculum are one and the same. Our intention is to interpret the 'wholeness' of the teaching and learning situation from the valuative standards embodied in traditions of classroom practice.

In this second phase we meet many of the arguments put forth in Chapter 6. Again, it is necessary to stress that it is important to be able to argue from the strong position of practice. Our position views the criteria for establishing rational action in both content and materials development as the social products of those involved with this development, and therefore depends upon both the specific context in which development occurs as well as the way in which the activity proceeds. To live out the meaning of this belief teachers must involve themselves with theoretical and practical development in this extended sense.

Before listing the activities and experiences which make up this second phase, it is necessary to recall our distinction between a 'resource' and an 'educational design'. The term resource has been used to convey the idea of 'one of a stock that can be drawn on' – that is, the teacher has an element of choice in selecting the resource which fits into a larger plan. Although this 'resource' may have encapsulated within its own structure an 'educational design', it is the teacher who chooses to stress or ignore this structure. Resources permit a flexibility of use. An 'educational design', on the other hand, represents a unit which is self-contained and self-consistent. Its structure, when

accepted in use, details the proceedings of the classroom. Since prescriptions are contained within the design, it foreshadows expected
outcomes brought about through implementing the design. Teachers
and students, in theory, have far less influence over classroom events,
as the 'design' represents a 'validated' strategy which ensures that
learning will occur when classroom events follow the course of the
design. By ignoring the prescriptive aspects of a design it is possible
for teachers to use parts of the materials as educational resources.

In the list of activities and experiences which follows, the suggestion
is to use, wherever appropriate, 'educational designs' as they were
intended – that is, to experience using a professional design product
in the prescribed manner under the prescribed conditions. Your role
will, therefore, be prescribed as a part of the design.

A reasonable experiential base would seem to be provided by:

Using Educational Designs (Software)

(1)   To have 'used' or provided for students to use the following
software:
      (a) an instructional television programme,
      (b) a slide-tape presentation,
      (c) an instructional audio-tape or audio-tutorial,
      (d) an instructional film (16mm or 8 mm).
(2)   To have used as a teaching or learning resource:
      (a) a single still visual – examples include slides, prints, wall
charts, models.
(3)   To have used a commercially prepared 'learning design' such as:
      (a) a programmed learning text or similar programmed
sequence,
      (b) a game or simulation,
      (c) a computer programme, either computer-assisted instruc-
tion where there is minimum involvement of the pupil in
determining the sequence of instruction, or computer-supported
instruction where more complex interactions between the
learner and the computer occur.
      (d) a curriculum package which prescribes a variety of audio-
visual aids and their 'mix' in the instructional process.
(4)   To have used a series of resources which have been designed
for flexible and adaptive use.

Using Audio-visual 'Playback' Hardware

To be familiar with the operation of:

(1)   a video-tape recorder (playback mode) with associated monitor/receiver TV,

(2)   8-mm and 16-mm movie projectors,

(3)   35-mm still projectors and associated dissolve units,

(4)   audio-tape cassette recorders/amplifiers/equalisers (playback mode), language 'labs',

(5)   overhead projectors,

(6)   opaque projectors,

(7)   video-disc systems.

Using Audio-visual 'Production' Hardware

To be familiar with the operation of:

(1)   a video camera, video-tape recorder, monitor/receiver (record mode),

(2)   a two-camera video system and switching device,

(3)   microphones, mixing and equalisation equipment for sound recording,

(4)   35-mm reflex cameras,

(5)   enlargers and darkroom equipment such as developing tanks, timers, bulk-film loaders, drum processors,

(6)   8-mm (home market) and 16-mm (non-electric drive) movie cameras,

(7)   simple film-cutting devices (8-mm and 16-mm) and editing equipment,

(8)   process cameras (or similar) for reduction/enlargement,

(9)   lettering devices including photographic lettering machines,

(10)   reprographic equipment - spirit and ink duplicators, offset duplicators, photostat machines,

(11)   'heat-copier' thermofax machines.

Using 'Production' Software – Raw Materials

To be able to select and load ready for production:

(1)   video-tapes (cassette and reel-to-reel systems),

(2)   audio-tape - various types with correct bias settings,

(3)   different film types (roll, cassette) of different characteristics (speed, daylight/tungsten) for 35-mm cameras,

(4)   appropriate filters for 35-mm cameras,

(5)   different film types for 8-mm and 16-mm cameras,

(6)   grades of photographic papers and matching, photographic solutions for photographic print production (black and white and colour),

(7)   suitable developing equipment for colour-film processing,

(8)   photographic materials for lettering machines and process cameras (photo-mechanical transfer process),

(9)   stencils, papers (and other surfaces) for reprographic equipment,

(10)   facsimile stencils and 'heat' transparencies for thermofax machines.

'Production' Hardware and Software – Associated Processes

To be able to:

(1)   connect cables to operate components of a 'video system',

(2)   carry out simple dubbing and editing procedures using two video-tape recorders,

(3)   use a two-light-source system to illuminate a simple make-shift studio for television production,

(4)   record 'off-air' (sound and video) using a VTR and receiver/ monitor,

(5)   connect cables to operate the components of an audio system – e.g. equaliser, microphones, auxiliary input, amplifier, mixer.

Design and Production Tasks

(1)   Take a topic that you are familiar with and structure a series of lessons around that topic. Decide upon the 'aims' of the series of lessons and establish methodological approaches. On completion of this sequence ask students to speculate upon your 'aims' and interpret your methodology.

(2)   Carry out two descriptive exercises:

(a) obtain materials from a curriculum project and use an inventory to check off its characteristics,

(b) obtain a 'description of teaching' inventory (skills analysis, style analysis or similar) and ask a friend to rate your performance or obtain a video-tape of the performance.

For both exercises, discuss the assumptions behind the various 'descriptive' categories and decide whether such 'objective' guides are of use.

(3)   Find out about the 'rational' curriculum development model. Take a six-week block of work in a subject area and attempt to use the model to generate an approach. Attempt to write behavioural objectives and carry out assessment using the behaviours as criteria.

(4)   Find out whether the administration of your school favours

norm-referenced or criterion-referenced measures. If they are sympathetic to criterion-referenced measures point out that:

(a) some students will probably meet the requirements on a first try,

(b) the other students, due to recycling and diagnostic help, will eventually reach the set criteria.

As a consequence of (a) and (b) all students in the class will be assigned the same grade-level, mark or percentage. Ask whether the administration will allow or support this situation if it were to occur in your classroom.

(5)   Carry out a historical exercise on the changes in the curriculum for your specialist-subject area. Who controls such change? (Or to put this another way, who defines and legitimates which content is to be introduced, retained or deleted?) What is the purpose behind and reasons given to justify such change? Is it possible to decide whether any one curriculum is better than another?

(6)   Curriculum is supposed to be 'socially valued knowledge, skills and attitudes'. If your school has a prescribed curriculum which encompasses a number of discrete subject areas try to carry out the following:

(a) an analysis of your own lesson materials, methodology and classroom style,

(b) observation of lessons in the other subject areas which go to make up the curriculum.

Now ask the following questions of yourself:

(i)   From an analysis of the content of your lessons, is it possible to identify any person, specialist group, or larger societal group that would 'socially value' the content of your lessons?

(ii) Do you personally value the content of your lessons? Why?

(iii) Did your methodological approach and classroom style also convey 'socially valued' attitudes?

(iv) Is it possible to identify any person, specialist group, or larger societal group that would 'socially value' your methodological approach and classroom style?

(v)   From your observation of other teachers pose similar questions to those in (i) to (iv).

(7)   Produce a range of materials to supplement a series of lessons for use in your classroom.

(8)   Produce one assemblage of materials on film or television and use this in your classroom.

(9)   Take one of your productions – say either (7) or (8) – and ask

another teacher to use the materials for his own purpose. Ask if you can observe the way in which the materials are used, or if this is not possible, question the teacher on the 'worth' of your materials.

(10)   Submit a design (either teaching or learning materials) and make a request to the 'production staff' of your school to produce your materials.

(11)   Ask another teacher to show you some of his/her materials that he/she has designed, and attempt to criticise or change this design without knowledge of the specific context for which this design was constructed.

These are but some suggestions which might influence the development of a personal practice-theory dialectic. And it is this personal development, that is, teacher development, which is at the heart of educational design. In a very real sense curriculum development and instructional-materials development are meaningful only in so far as they describe teacher development. For in the last analysis it is the teacher who translates any design, be it his own or a professional product, into action; it is upon the basis of teacher judgements that educational encounters develop and 'classroom life' proceeds.

Now there are various constraints acting upon the development of a personal practice-theory dialectic. Such constraints can be seen in terms of the power relationships within the classroom, the school, schooling and society. One way of facing the implications of these power relations is to seek personal answers to three questions: What do I understand by the term learning? What do I understand the function of schooling to be? What do I understand learning and schooling to be in terms of the school in which I am teaching?

The final chapter attempts to give further information which might influence answers to these three questions, and so introduce alternative approaches to educational design.

8 ALTERNATIVES IN EDUCATIONAL DESIGN

One of the most difficult aspects of this final chapter is to be able to write in a non-prescriptive fashion yet be 'positive' in suggesting alternatives in educational design. Our approach so far has been to attempt to weld doing and thinking about educational design. Because of the vulnerability of teachers in this area an important part of countering educational design has been to sensitise and provide arguments against the metaphors and ideological values held by professional designers. So far much of this counter has been defensive in spirit, and it is now time to gain the offensive.

As we have already seen, the basis of our offensive is to assert, with confidence, a set of values which oppose the two fundamental values of the management ideology. Thus, our offensive requires further philosophical analysis and practical action within the ideological framework used by teachers.

The Ideological Framework of Teachers

What are the features of the ideological framework used by teachers? Wolcott (1977), in defining teacher culture in terms of an ideational system, identifies five key features: teachers are autonomous, teaching is sacrosanct, only teachers understand teaching, teaching has a tradition not easily changed, and teachers are vulnerable. These features are in part the result of a 'means-oriented' style – the diffuse and sometimes contradictory elements within this 'culture' are evident, as teachers often cannot agree upon a course of action for a given situation.

In a previous chapter the idea of tradition was linked with how groups value things from special viewpoints. That is 'traditional action' is based upon evaluating a situation in terms of a set of values. Those values which lie at the very heart of this system of values not only fulfil a prime 'valuative' role, but can also be used to identify the social group which applies them. Such values have been termed core values.

Clearly, core-values and other complimentary values have an ideological function – they have a dual aspect of 'meaning or sense-making', as well as providing a way of furthering or maintaining the interests of

109

the group and its members. So, to delineate the features of 'teacher-culture' we need to identify the core values held by teachers. However, for our purposes it is not necessary to be able to identify all the core values, and we need consider only those which impinge upon the area of educational design.

Practical Knowledge and Practical Reasoning

One of the first and most obvious core values is concerned with how teachers value 'knowledge' as it concerns their functioning as teachers. The issue is perennial. How do teachers in training learn to teach? (Through traditional methods of induction into skilful activities such as apprenticeship or through a knowledge of theoretical matters based upon contributory disciplines?) Is there an art of teaching but a science of learning? Are teachers born, not made?

This issue is also a feature of teacher talk. For teachers in training teaching practice is always valued higher than their theoretical studies – and, often, the advice of supervisory teachers to such students upon entering a school is to 'forget all you have previously been told at the teacher training institution and begin to learn from doing and watching'. Rarely will a 'theory' learnt at a teacher training institution be cited by a teacher as a way of justifying the activities of day-to-day classroom life; most of the theoretical indoctrination of teacher training institutions is destined to obscurity. Practical knowledge and practical reasoning hold sway within the act of teaching.

In this way teachers rightly claim that only teachers understand teaching. The exclusiveness of this position is a function of this emphasis upon practical knowledge – practical knowledge has immediacy and involves purposes, and as Wolcott says, 'either one is teaching or one is no longer a teacher'.

So, one of the foremost and obvious core values relates to knowledge claims. It is not surprising then that teachers reject the professionals' notion of educational design, as it is based on a value which is diametrically opposed to a teacher core value. Teachers highly value skills and craft knowledge derived from their traditions of practice or through intuitive means!

Means-oriented Description and Explanation

Support for the teacher core value is provided by an alternative philo-sophical position which is 'means oriented' and fundamentally con-cerned with *human* meaning. Perhaps an example will make this clearer. You are gossiping about Mr X 'behind his back' with a group of friends. Mr X is about to enter the room and is spotted by one of the group, who coughs. Now within this group the coughing is a warning to be careful about what is being said or to change the subject. To Mr X it is just a cough. The point of all this is that the explanations given con-cerning this coughing can be quite different - according to Mr X the person had a throat irritation, but for a member of the group coughing is explained in terms of its meaning as a warning.

These two forms of explanation occur in practical situations invol-ving classroom action. An event might be explained in terms of *process* - i.e. in a way which attempts to extract 'purposes' from the explana-tion. Thus, the event is explained in terms of abstract, impersonal and external causes in a fashion termed 'scientific'. The other way is to centre upon purpose and see explanation invested with human meanings. In this way objects and people are 'cultural' and are not viewed as things. Objects, people and events become cultural data all saturated with 'meaning', and description and explanations are in terms of *praxis* rather than process.

Now the concept of praxis is used in different days by different writers. One of the clearest outlines of usage which suits our purposes is given by Ingleby (1972),

> While process describes the behaviour of inanimate objects, accounted for wholly by causes, praxis is the medium of the specifi-cally human: it implies behaviour which is purposive and account-able for only in terms of its meaningfulness (whatever may be said about its 'causes'). . .
>
> A piece of praxis is defined in terms of its intended end, the end being a project achieved or a message communicated: the means to this end (movements or symbols) are always determined by the context (a situation and/or code), and cannot be seen as meaningful without reference to this context.'

This notion challenges the mode of description and explanation put forth by 'process' approaches, and contends that areas such as perception, understanding, meaning-making, communicating, thinking and reasoning are identified primarily by the operation of praxis. Therefore, approaches built upon 'process' models are fundamentally inadequate in dealing with these areas. For example, 'process' models of human information processing which liken the perception-cognition-memory and retrieval aspects of learning to computer 'systems', are not only useless for explaining instruction and human interaction, but worse, promote a false view of such things. Likewise, behaviourism is found conceptually deficient.

Given that such notions expose deficiencies, or at least seriously challenge orthodoxies, the obvious question arises: Why do such movements as behaviourism, information processing, and indeed the whole technological-rational approach in education, persist? Attempts to answer such questions soon scratch political beliefs!

Another type of defence of the 'means-oriented style' is provided by extending our arguments borrowed from Oakeshott (1962) and Polanyi (1962). Our earlier excursions into using the philosophical positions of these writers were quite limited, and it is now time to extend some of these ideas.

So far, we have looked at two types of 'rules' which support activity. Operative rules are 'technical' in the sense that they are entirely dependent upon some theoretical knowledge. The best examples are provided by the types of rules which are derived from theories which are able to describe, explain and predict. Scientific theories, for example, allow the generation of operative rules which take the form: 'to cause x to happen, you must do y'. Within education such 'rules' are generally far less 'causal' since they are derived from 'theory' which usually cannot satisfy the conditions of explanation and prediction. Nevertheless, such precepts are often put in a 'scientific' fashion in the hope that the form of the statement will lend authority to its substance.

Normative rules, on the other hand, are concerned with the establishment of types and standards of behaviour reflecting either activity-based traditions or philosophical stances. Such precepts consider what is appropriate (or what ought to happen) in a situation. Normative precepts are considered while an activity or mode of conduct is being carried out. The final judgement of what constitutes the 'best way of proceeding' rests in a balancing of a number of normative and operational considerations which are to be considered contextually.

So, practical action might be viewed as the result of 'balancing' such operative and normative rules; thus, practical action could be explained in terms of the way in which such considerations are 'balanced'. Now it is possible to argue that a further set of rules can guide this 'bringing together' of normative and operative rules – but then it is also possible that an even more powerful set of rules are required to detail when and how the new rules are to be used! Clearly, there are serious deficiencies with this account of action.

Tacit Integration

Polanyi, on the other hand, contends that this bringing together, balancing or to use his term, integration, can be tacit. That is, we are unable to state the 'rules'. Put briefly, we know more than we can tell! We therefore possess another type of 'awareness' that we bring to bear upon solving practical problems – an awareness which defies explicit specification. Knowing the explicit normative and operative rules brings an 'explicit awareness' to the problem and, as Polanyi points out, this type of awareness of the rules of an activity often proves an insufficient base for 'doing' an activity. 'Doing', in its most complete sense, involved a 'tacit' or unspecifiable component.

Consequently, knowing how to proceed with educational design in a given situation does not entirely depend upon knowing rules. Indeed, Polanyi's interest in the area of 'knowing' stems from the well-known fact that the aim of a skilful performance is achieved by the observance of a set of rules which are *not known as such* to the person following them. Examples of such performances range from riding a bicycle, wool-classing, ballet dancing, being a scientist, to acupuncture and television production. Rules about such performances may even be explicitly stated and written down, but their integration into practice remains tacit. Thus, one can be given explicit procedures for driving a car in a motor manual, baking a cake in a cook book or carrying out sexual intercourse in a sex manual, yet not achieve the integration into practice which is necessary to allow one to say that one is a good driver, cook or lover.

The explicit knowledge provided by maxims, rules and theories serves as a guide only if it can be integrated into the practical knowledge of the art. To ask the question of which knowledge is more important or more fundamental is, in part, to miss the point – both forms of knowing and awareness are generally used. However, Polanyi believes that we must eventually side with practitioners, as he claims that while tacit knowledge may be possessed by itself, explicit knowledge must rely upon being tacitly understood. Thus, all knowledge is either tacit, or rooted in tacit knowledge.

An important consequence of Polanyi's work is that it makes the issue of 'how things are learnt' problematic. His philosophy forces the following question: Does what is to be learned determine how things are learned? The designer, on the other hand, assumes that his 'process approach' is suited to all learning; the techniques of educational technology and curriculum design are content-independent. Production of learning or curriculum materials follows from feeding content through a process 'machine' so that a refined product is produced!

To see why this assumption of content-independence is so important let us assume the opposite to be the case. That is, how things are learnt (which necessarily involves design decisions) are totally content-dependent. Educational design would therefore be controlled by subject and not 'process' experts. Each subject would have appropriate design procedures which are drawn from an appreciation of the content of the subject, and design would therefore be considered a part of the methodology of the subject. At the teacher training level, instead of courses in educational technology or curriculum, each of the subject disciplines would offer educational design within courses of history methods, geography methods, science methods and the like. Clearly, without the assumption of the content-independence of design processes the professional designer's role is threatened.

Now design can appear to be a content-independent activity. This appearance is based upon a conception of knowing which stresses the receiving of rule-based information. In terms of Polanyi's analysis this form of knowing is incomplete and requires tacit integration for understanding and application. A further point is that the high tacit component of some types of knowing means that relying upon explicit instructional procedures and materials may be inappropriate. This applies to many skills: how much of learning to play golf, wool-classing, using chopsticks, vegetable gardening, or snow skiing (for example) can be taught through the explicit instructional procedures within learning materials?

Knowing, in its fullest sense, cannot be content-independent. Where education aims at appreciation, understanding or insight these abilities are highly content-dependent. We talk of historical understanding, scientific insight or musical appreciation. But, in reality, designers cannot offer such aims. Their ideological position is rooted in explicit and rule-based information which is expressed through behaviours. Their beliefs exclude such sensitivity to the content-dependent nature of knowing; theirs is an impoverished framework which requires dismantling.

Polanyi's work suggests several other points concerning the practice of educational design. First, and foremost, practical knowledge is to be highly valued; theoretic knowledge is useful to the extent that it can be integrated into practice. This means that teachers are in a unique position with regard to designing for teaching and learning within their schools, as the practice of educational design relies heavily upon practical contextual knowledge. Secondly, the fact that teachers cannot always articulate the reasons for their actions with regard to decisions about educational design for their classrooms is, according to this viewpoint, to be expected. This is due to the tacit component of knowledge. Thirdly, the traditions of classroom practice provide guidance in interpreting present practice – in fact, part of learning about educational design involves experiencing this tradition so that its valuative aspects can be applied to specific circumstances. It is important to realise that traditions are not fully articulated – in this way groups that apply a tradition are constantly reinterpreting elements of the tradition so that it might serve to direct current practice. Instead of denigrating the role of tradition within classroom practice, educationists should be working to understand its function!

Educational designers seek to destroy this teacher tradition. In order to establish thier own technological-rational 'tradition' they ridicule aspects of teacher practice in the area of design. Usually, this is done by taking some event or procedure out of context and establishing its 'meaning' from *their* 'meaning-making' ideology. Consequently, such events or procedures seem, at best, *ad hoc*, or, at worst, senseless!

Control Over Teaching and Learning

Let us now return to establishing another of the core values of 'teacher-culture'. To go back to the recurring themes in teacher talk mentioned by Wolcott, a second value is derived from the notion that 'teaching is sacrosanct'.

Teachers are inducted into a tradition which views teaching in the classroom as the single most important aspect of their role. Events or actions which interfere or place limitations upon teaching are challenged. Teachers guard jealously the authority they derive from being at the 'chalk face'; in their view authority exerted from bureaucratic or from organisational structures within education authorities should not interfere with classroom events. Classroom events are interpreted through teacher values, and not those of bureaucracy or management.

Thus, teachers attempt to prevent any interference with teaching. They well realise that direct interferences in terms of lesson-by-lesson or day-by-day control is virtually impossible, and attempts at control must therefore be engineered from outside the classroom. And one avenue of control which eventually works down to the level of 'class-room life' is through educational design. Consequently, teachers prefer not to employ the jargon and concepts of educational design, and instead emphasise alternative ideas which support their conception of their role within the classroom. We therefore find that teachers employ the idea of preparation rather than detailed, long-term planning, and support this emphasis by stressing the fact that classroom life requires a flexible approach which responds to the needs and interests of children. Obviously, teachers do engage in 'long-term' planning but, as a political act, they prefer to stress the immediate in the form of short-term preparation. Preparation presents far less possibilities for external control!

So, the value position that teaching is sacrosanct generates a number of consistent values. One such value is the teacher-preference of 'pre paration' over 'planning' - or, to put it a stronger way, educational design in the form of long-term planning is to be rejected. Teachers stress the 'wholeness' of the teaching and learning 'totality' as a contrast to the educational designer's separation of design and execution. 'Wholeness' in teacher terms can be expressed only through the myriad of elements which influence preparation. The designer's view of 'wholeness' as expressed through the systems approach is an example of 'ecological irrelevance' - it says little about, and is rarely useful in describing, classroom life. Decisions about 'wholeness', in the teacher's view, can be made only through reference to 'thick' descriptions of the immediate situation and context. The systems-styled thinking of the educational designer does not relate to what teachers call 'wholeness'.

Change and Tradition

Our discussion of the values within 'teacher culture' has indicated the fundamental importance of the concept of tradition. In Chapter 6, where we were concerned with the theoretical arguments which might be used to counter educational design, we used this concept to establish a meaning for 'rational action'. And now, within our concern for alternative practices, we again find the concept of tradition playing a central role. For many educationists interested in alternatives and change the notion of 'tradition' provides a stumbling block; tradition is linked with conservative doctrines and is therefore incompatible with alternative approaches.

For example, if we accept the idea that an activity like educational design cannot be specified in detail, and consequently cannot be transmitted by prescription, then we move to the position that 'submission' to the traditions of practice is necessary if an 'apprentice' is to learn from a 'master'. As Polanyi (1962) puts it, the hidden rules of an art 'can only be assimilated by a person who surrenders himself to that extent uncritically to the imitation of another'. Critics point out the basic conservatism in this 'socialisation process'. The argument, they contend, is but an apology for 'professionalism'. Under such conditions practical action becomes rigidly confined to traditional practice, thus limiting or even excluding change.

Such arguments have superficial appeal – however, they hinge around a concept of tradition which supports their conclusions. Here, tradition is portrayed as a fixed body of belief which has ossified – such beliefs are 'backward looking' and, in attempting to value the present through the values of the past, are out of step with the needs of the present. When cast in such terms is there little wonder that the charge of 'conservatism' is heard!

But this conception is challenged by many sociologists and anthropologists. To them a tradition is highly malleable, and allows each group to select and evaluate elements of the tradition to suit current needs. This dynamism associated with traditions reflects the social nature of a tradition. As Smolicz (1975) states:

> tradition cannot be regarded as simply any type of link between the past and the present – it cannot be submitted to mechanically and unthinkingly – but demands an active display of the sentiments of acceptance or rejection. Thus it cannot be accounted for without reference to the phenomena of human consciousness.

Such notions of tradition have little trouble in accounting for 'evolutionary' change. But how can such notions be compatible with revolutionary change?

It is difficult to answer such a question in a direct fashion. Critics of the notion of tradition point to the fact that traditions are involved with preservation; revolutions, on the other hand, uproot existing orders and beliefs. To answer such critics it would seem that we would need to give an example of an area where tradition plays a fundamental role, yet does not appear to hinder revolution.

Such an area exists. It is the area of scientific knowledge! Traditions in scientific areas are known as paradigms. Paradigms, as traditions, are never fully articulated, and the quest for articulation within the precise ground rules of the paradigm has been termed 'normal science'. According to Kuhn (1969) it is this restriction of scope provided by a tradition which may even assist revolutionary change.

> Given a generation in which to effect the change, individual rigidity is compatible with a community that can switch from paradigm to paradigm when the occasion demands. Particularly, it is compatible when that very rigidity provides the community with a sensitive indicator that something has gone wrong.

This does not mean that scientific change and educational change are necessarily similar – instead, it points to the idea that explanations of change which employ the concept of tradition are not necessarily excluded from 'explanations' of revolutionary change. Consequently, possibilities for both evolutionary and revolutionary change can arise from within a tradition.

An understanding of the way in which 'teacher tradition' influences judgements within the classroom is of utmost importance. Classroom life is the living out of the meanings and values embodied in teacher tradition – it displays the active evaluations which result from applying the tradition to specific circumstances. However, the influence of the shared meanings and values of a tradition normally operate at an acritical level. Consequently, traditions create an 'environment' which is so much taken for 'granted' that the environment itself becomes almost 'invisible' to those who live within it. This invisibility is a result of ideological saturation and so complete is this saturation that it provides the very 'commonsense' reasons for action within the environment.

Often such environments only become 'visible' when shared assumptions are violated, or when changing circumstances cause individuals or groups to revalue parts of a tradition. This visibility of meanings and values is connected with change or adjustment. Consequently, a sensitising to the images, values and structures of environments is a fundamental precursor to change.

Negotiation

So far we have looked at the classroom environment as it affects educational design exclusively from a teacher viewpoint. This has been quite intentional, as it is important that the teacher becomes aware of the 'hidden agendas' which he or she transmits through structuring and implementing teaching and learning. It is now time to focus upon the students within the 'classroom environment'.

Our stance concerning 'rational action' placed central importance upon evaluation of 'on-going' activity. What happens 'next' in the classroom is a function of students' reactions, activities and interests to what is now occurring. Thus, students and teachers engage in 'encounters' which influence design decisions. In this way a teacher's planning or educational design is 'negotiated' by students and teacher.

Thus, the 'classroom floor' idea of educational design must incorporate a flexibility which allows 'negotiation'. This idea is nothing new – teachers include both planning and preparation within their concept of educational design. Planning describes broad aims – it is content oriented because it is through the content that 'encounters' may be specified. Preparation describes the immediate possibilities for student-teacher interaction – it is not divorced from planning yet is responsive to the outcomes of preceding 'encounters'. Preparation often involves looking for specific relevant resources, dealing with organisational problems, providing for group interactions.

To characterise preparation as *ad hoc*, pragmatic, unsystematic or unconnected is to view such decisions in isolation. Decisions at this level are the translation of values (which underlie planning) into practice. Such decisions are not based upon infinitely elastic criteria; instead, they represent the 'living out' of the values and power relations within the classroom.

Now, as has been previously pointed out, this 'living out' of the classroom interaction is carried out within certain constraints. The very fact that teachers teach in schools and participate in 'institutionalised' education restricts the 'living out' process. Planning and preparation are limited by such constraints; teachers and students operate within a special 'world view' which 'makes sense' of such constraints. The reality of such 'world views' cannot be doubted. Both teachers and students can accurately describe their circumstance in terms of the 'collection of values' they work within.

The practice of alternatives in educational design involves describing this 'world view', and exploring within it ways in which an alternative practice-theory dialectic can be achieved. There can be no prescriptions for the actual development along such pathways in educational design. However, one thing remains clear – our conception of rational action within the teaching and learning process means that students both *create*, and interact with, educational design. This is an inescapable conclusion of our description of teaching and learning – it is also a concrete feeling of those who participate upon the classroom floor!

So what can be said to assist the practice of alternatives in design. It is clear that we cannot give formulae or prescriptions, as our analysis has led us to a much more complex interpretation of educational design. It is this very interpretation which precludes the tidy pseudo-rational description of the professional designer. Our interpretation is unavoidably political, does not treat design as a 'technology', and is ideologically based; as the introductory chapter hinted, it establishes a reconceptualisation of the idea of design based upon a personal solution to classroom design problems. Consequently, the closest that we can approach to assist in the practice of alternatives is to list some of the factors which may influence practical action.

These are to:

(1)   work within the school either as a self-sufficient individual or form a collective styled or 'non-managed' unit with other teachers;

(2)   carry out curriculum and materials design within the political, organisational and economic constraints of the school, subject department or group of schools. Since such constraints are often ill-defined it is possible to argue for considerable change in practice yet still work from within the school structures;

(3)   analyse the 'power structure' of the school in relation to control over the 'instruments of production'. Try to influence the administration to change to an open-access policy for both equipment and production materials. Collective action by teachers could decide materials allocation;

(4)   become involved in subject committees and library-resource committees in order to monitor and influence purchases of equipment and packaged curricula;

(5)   work with other teachers who are skilled in curriculum and materials design;

(6)   try different 'power-sharing' arrangements with students. This can be approached by taking an open-ended approach to a topic and negotiating with students their learning in this area. Design for such

an area may be the working out by students and yourself of a number of expressive objectives which describe features of educational encounters but leave outcomes open;

(7)   try to find ways in which students' critical comments of their work can be included within your evaluation.

These are but some of the more obvious suggestions which might assist in the generation of alternative practices. The importance of this task cannot be understated – without active teacher involvement in design the way is open to a complete 'take-over' of this area by professional designers.

Examples of Alternative Practices within Teacher Training

Many teacher training awards offer courses in educational technology and curriculum design. Such courses are 'process oriented' and are concerned with issues common to many subject areas ranging from methodological topics such as discipline to curriculum-design processes. Sometimes courses are structured around focal issues – for example, a focus upon materials production which spills over into methodological and curricular issues, or a curriculum-design focus which widens to consider materials production and classroom methodology. Often, in more traditional institutions these 'process-oriented' matters are considered within subject boundaries, and consequently it is subject content which integrates the other issues. The following course is fundamentally different, in conception and style, from such 'methods' courses.

A Tutorial Course in Media for Classroom Teaching and Learning

The author has conducted this course for first-year students in a teacher training award. As students have had little experience in viewing teaching/learning processes as 'teachers', one of the first steps in the tutorial course is to provide initial experiences in the use of media for classroom teaching and learning. Students were issued with a handbook which explains the teaching and learning style of the tutorials. Sections of the handbook illustrate this process.

Exhibit A: Handbook Material

Introduction (from the course handbook)
Talking about educational technology achieves little – writing about

it, probably even less! If educational technology has any meaning at all it is in terms of techniques, actions, and activities which assist classroom teaching and learning.

This tutorial course will attempt to locate such techniques, actions and activities as responses to 'realistic' problems of classroom teaching and learning. Now it is impossible to achieve this sort of ideal. Yes, it is true that courses such as this cannot accurately reflect all the realities of classroom life; yes, it is true that there will be an element of artificiality in what we attempt to do; yes, it is true that our description of classroom life will be somewhat idealised and the actions we will be suggesting represent what we feel *ought* to happen; and yes, it is true that behind such techniques, actions and activities lies a particular idea about teaching and learning. And such techniques, actions and activities are not 'neutral' and can be evaluated from political, social, practical, economic (to name but a few) viewpoints.

The tutorial course looks at those techniques, actions and activities which employ *media* for classroom teaching and learning. An important aspect of this is to introduce skills which can be used to assist teaching and learning tasks – how do you produce print materials?; just how do you take photographs?; how are overhead projectors used in the classroom?, can you produce a short T.V. programme in a school setting?

This course is not aimed at producing learning packages of a type similar to those available commercially. Many teachers have rejected this form of learning package. Instead we aim to provide skills which enable teachers to supplement and enrich their classroom teaching.

A Tentative Plan

As a tutor I've had to ask myself:
  Why am I teaching this to you?
  How should I teach this?

My answers are:
There exists a body of techniques and skills relating to media which form *part* of the repertoire of skills that teachers use in negotiating classroom life. Such skills enable teachers to achieve other objectives such as motivating students, presenting information and the like. There is a wealth of teacher testimony to the fact that these techniques and the media can assist teaching and learning. Also,

the production of teaching and learning aids is an essential and creative part of the teaching and learning process. Consequently, imparting such skills and techniques is a necessary preparation for teachers in training.

There are many ways in which such skills and information might be covered. The approach that I would like to use is to 'negotiate' such activities in response to a 'simulation' of a classroom problem. Perhaps an example will make this clearer. Suppose an initial situation of *using* an existing audio-visual aid is agreed upon. A group may search out an audio tape, a slide-set (or similar) and attempt to *use* the materials upon the tutorial class. In this way, from the basis of experience in a 'simulated' situation, we can make critical comments about the strengths and weaknesses of the materials and the methodological aspects associated with using such materials. Now let us assume that we were not completely satisfied with the materials. We might then decide that further production is required to suit our particular purposes – perhaps more of the same media, or perhaps adjunct materials using another medium. To carry out such production certain skills will be required – so, there will be the need to investigate the equipment and materials necessary.

In this way we can investigate production possibilities. Clearly, there will be decisions to be made concerning the scope (do we consider all the media?) and the depth (do we spend more time on X rather than Y?) to which we investigate production possibilities. Without being prescriptive, I anticipate that we may consider *three* production possibilities and carry out productions in these areas. As well as this we will meet a number of other problems such as objectives, planning techniques, and evaluation.

So, my answer to the second question is that you and I will be involved in considering a 'simulated' classroom life situation. Arising from the *use* of media and materials you may decide to supplement, (or re-design) this approach – this decision involves the application of skills and techniques.

As tutor, I hope to be able to guide the acquisition of skills and techniques and influence your discussions on production.

So that you can select a particular 'experience', the range of skills and a developmental approach to using them is outlined later in this booklet. The two possible approaches to the tutorial productions both employ a cycle of use, critical analysis, design – the first approach applies this cycle to a *single* starting simulation, while the second uses three smaller starting situations. Expressed in the form of diagrams the possibilities are

First Approach

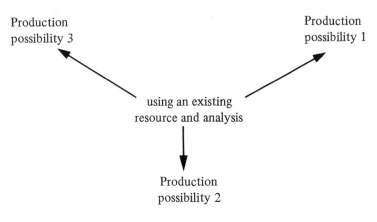

Production
possibility 3

Production
possibility 1

using an existing
resource and analysis

Production
possibility 2

Second Approach

Medium 1	Use & Analysis	Leads to ⟶	Production in Medium 1
Medium 2	Use & Analysis	Leads to ⟶	Production in Medium 2
Medium 3	Use & Analysis	Leads to ⟶	Production in Medium 3

Both of these approaches will be discussed in tutorials.

Another question that I must ask myself is:

  How will I know whether my teaching and your learning has been successful?

My answer to this question is:

In any classroom teachers make judgements upon the processes which occur and the products which are produced. Now in this tutorial course certain processes are easily identifiable – for example, you should know how to use equipment and materials (irrespective of the actual product). Other classroom processes such as 'communication', 'involvement' *etc.* are far more difficult to gauge and although these are of prime importance they will not feature within my *formal* assessment.

Judgements about products are a little easier to deal with – at least the products themselves are 'concrete' and can be subjected to extended critical scrutiny. Thus your reported reasons for a production and the actual production, form important products which can be evaluated.

So, my evaluation of the tutorial course will consist of

(a)   satisfactory performance in skills area – this can be carried out within the tutorial sessions as and when the skills arise or in the normal equipment testing periods.

(b)   getting you to keep a folder of 'products' which arise from the tutorial sessions – such a folder might include written work, observations of lessons, materials that have been produced, critical comments, etc.

A Course Unit in Curriculum Design

Another example of alternatives in action is taken from a course in curriculum design. In Chapter 7, where the practical issues of countering educational design were considered, one of the means of 'consciousness-raising' with regard to analysing the underlying values lived out in terms of personal classroom practice, was to put three questions: What do I understand by the term learning? What do I understand the function of schooling to be? What do I understand learning and schooling to be in terms of the school in which I am teaching? Questions similar to these were put to teachers undertaking a unit in curriculum design with the intention that they could write their present 'answers' and be encouraged to write further on each of these issues as the course progressed. This proved a difficult exercise for many – indeed, most teachers would not hand in their initial thoughts claiming that their 'answers' were too vague or personally unsatisfactory. Some were afraid that they were being 'exposed' and required time to think out issues; others ran for the safety of text book 'definitions' feeling that they were not yet ready to 'personalise' such matters. Exhibit B illustrates a first response by a teacher to such issues.

Exhibit B
Facsimile Materials – Curriculum Design

What is learning?

At junior primary level learning is doing. It is being involved with various stimuli and reacting to them and with them. Education is finding out about the world through experiencing it, and finding out about people by mixing with them. Sometimes learning has to be rote when no practical experience can be engineered and it has also to be indoctrination.

What is Schooling?

The interaction between child and teacher and others. Setting up situations to help the child to develop self confidence. self-awareness, decision-making skills, social skills, appreciation of their environment and eventually the world environment.

It is also, by necessity, acquiring knowledge – not always relevant – values, and attitudes which society sees as important.

What is a Curriculum Document?

Curriculum is what happens in class between pupils and teacher. Curriculum committees assume teachers will use their materials. Curriculum (*sic*) are developed by teachers in classroom by their decisions to use/not use them; how they use them, etc. The curriculum statement is only a possible guide to what might develop in class. Decisions a teacher makes about curriculum depend on how useful she finds the materials, on her training, her view of the world and herself. The richness of her experiences will guide the quality of these decisions. Emphasis therefore on teacher development to change ideas, teaching styles, perceptions of what happens in her class situation.

The exhibits are but two fairly obvious ways of attempting alternative strategies in the area of educational design. As a first step the issues under investigation are made problematic. That is, teachers and trainee teachers are asked to 'become aware of' the basis of what they regarded as the 'common sense' of their practices or beliefs. Once this stage is reached opportunities for developing a personal 'practice-theory' sequence are negotiated.

The development of such alternative practices becomes all the more important when we consider the possible 'futures' in the areas associated with educational design.

Professionalised Design, Teaching and Learning

The visions of professional designers have been recently put in *Instructional Innovator*, a journal of the Association for Educational Communications and Technology. The challenge to classroom teaching and learning is clear – technology and educational design will radically change our conception of teaching and learning. Three comments by contributors to this edition highlight the concerns about educational design that have been expressed in this book – they concern cost-effectiveness, commercialisation of educational services and centralisation and control of knowledge.

According to Charles Blaschke (1980) (President of Education Turnkey Systems Inc. and Director of the Microcomputer Education Network),

> The cost-effectiveness and the feasibility of instructional media and technology for improving learning and developing skill have been clearly demonstrated in industry, military and other training environments. The problem is that the managerial and social environment in which a school system operates is not conducive to cost-effective applications of sophisticated media and technology systems.

Our concern is that schools, in response to the pressures for cost-effectiveness will adopt the procedures of professional designers and, in so doing, be pushed towards an 'environment' which, managerially and socially, is modelled upon a combination of industry, military and other training institutions.

The second comment, from Dean Jamison (1980) (a senior economist for The World Bank) concerns technological delivery. He writes:

> The most dramatic influence probably will be the reduced price of computer instruction. This will allow vendors of educational services to skip over the schools and reach learners directly – including adults who want to continue to learn. Improved technological delivery will create competition for traditional schools; it also will likely increase the amount of time people spend in learning.

Our concern has been that through educational design such vendors can structure educational services to present an essentially conservative viewpoint. The design promotes a view of education which is supportive to the role adopted by the educational vendor. This applies equally to design in the form of Disney materials as to computer games. The political implications of this development are made clearer in the third comment which is also from Jamison (1980),

> I believe the government, universities, and individual academics will continue in educational roles, but the private sector will have a greater investment in preparing media materials. You can't really expect a cottage industry approach to producing the more complicated computer-assisted instructional materials to work as successfully as it has in the preparation of text book.

Our concern has been for the 'centralisation' of knowledge and production and the resulting loss of freedom and role change this implies for teachers.

Whether all educational technologists and curriculum leaders realise that their role embodies management values is unimportant. The point is that, whether they are aware of it or not, their view of educational design serves a 'middle-management' function within some broader management structure. The question now becomes who manages the middle managers?

The analysis of the management ideology has purposely been confined to the middle-management level. To move outside of this boundary invites another journey over hazardous terrain: conspiracy theories, the political economy of education, education as a 'state apparatus', and cultural reproduction are but some of the more obvious obstacles.

In a very real sense the identification of ultimate managers is unimportant to the practical concerns of this book. Indeed, it is perhaps more important for teachers to realise that management over their actions is not necessarily immediate or through 'physical' means. Undoubtedly an understanding of how authority is distributed and invested within the larger institutionalised context is important, yet for practical classroom action it may be more useful to expose the management and control of action by the 'common-sense' categories created by the management ideology. As we have seen, where technological-rationality is seen as 'common-sense' there is a very real control over action.

This book has tried to expose both the idea control of middle managers and hint at the mind-control exerted by the management ideology. The counter-measures outlined are given in the belief that there is a political necessity for teachers to maintain control over educational design. This is imperative at two levels – within the education sub-culture and for society at large. If teaching and learning are to remain as vital, creative and adaptive processes the teacher should strive to maintain control over educational design; without this control teachers will lose out to professional designers who will turn them into instructors or presenters as part of an 'instructional delivery system'. If societies are to avoid the centralisation and standardisation of 'knowledge' (with their totalitarian overtones), educational design should not be entrusted to monoliths, state or private.

The suggestions to counter educational design are not necessarily anti-technology – indeed, many of the practical activities are concerned with ensuring that a practice-theory dialectic is developed in using technology in education. Alternative conceptions of design are essentially against a technological philosophy of education, and this is why much of this book has been concerned with philosophical issues.

In the final analysis it is the philosophical issues rather than the technical competencies which prove vital to establishing alternative conceptions of design. Such conceptions will not arise from mainstream curriculum or educational technology as these areas serve existing power structures. Alternatives in design depend upon rejecting the 'common-sense' structures of professionalised design which imply 'the superiority of the controllers over the controlled.' (Hamblin, 1974). And teachers, through developing a practice-theory dialectic which continually rejects this 'common-sense' assumption in both thinking and doing, can effectively counter educational design.

References

BLASCHKE, C. 'Can Instructional Media and Technology be Used to Improve Learning. How?' *Instructional Innovator*, vol 25, no. 2, (1980), p. 19

INGLEBY, D. 'Ideology and the Human Sciences: Some Comments on the Role of Reification in Psychology and Psychiatry' in Pateman, T. (ed), *Counter Course*, (Penguin, Harmondsworth, 1972)

HAMBLIN, A. C. *Evaluation and Control of Training*, (London, McGraw Hill, 1974), p. 186

JAMISON, D. 'What Factors Will Influence Education and Instructional Technology in the Future?', *Instructional Innovator*, vol. 25, no. 2, (1980), p. 23

KUHN, T. S. *The Structure of Scientific Revolutions*, Second Edition, (enlarged) (University of Chicago Press, Chicago, 1969)

OAKESHOTT, M. *Rationalism in Politics*, (Methuen, London, 1962)

POLANYI, M. *Personal Knowledge*, (London, Routledge & Kegan Paul, 1962), p. 53

SMOLICZ, J. J. 'The Concept of Tradition: A Humanistic Interpretation', *The Australian and New Zealand Journal of Sociology,* vol. 10, no. 2, (1975), pp. 75-83

WOLCOTT, H. F. *Teachers vs. Technocrats,* (Centre for Education Policy and Management, University of Oregon, 1977)

INDEX